RENEWALS 458-4574

DATE DUE

D1053288

GAYLORD

PRINTED IN U.S.A.

POLAND
UNDER BLACK LIGHT

Library
University of Texas
at San Antonio

via mail
Leroy
4 January 1989

Library
University of Texas
at San Antonio

Janusz Anderman

POLAND

UNDER BLACK LIGHT

With the author's new story from Warsaw

Introduction by Stanislaw Baranczak

**translated by
Nina Taylor and Andrew Short**

readers international

The title of this book in Polish is *Brak tchu,* first published in Polish
by PULS Publications, London, September 1983.
Copyright © PULS Publications 1983.
"Jakoś pusto" appeared in PULS 24, Winter 1984-85.
Copyright © PULS Publications 1985.

First published in English by Readers International, Inc., London and
New York, whose editorial branch is at 8 Strathray Gardens,
London NW3 4NY, Great Britain. US/Canadian inquiries to
Subscriber Service Department, P.O. Box 959, Columbia,
Louisiana 71418 USA.

English translation copyright © Readers International, Inc. 1985.

Cover illustration, "A Look into Another World",
by Jerzy Czerniawski, Warsaw.
Courtesy of Städtische Bühnen Münster, FRG
Design by Jan Brychta
Typeset by Grassroots Typeset, London NW6
Printed and bound in Great Britain by Richard Clay
(The Chaucer Press) Ltd., Bungay, Suffolk
ISBN 0-930523-13-X hardcover
ISBN 0-930523-14-8 paperback

CONTENTS

Introduction

One of the stories in the present collection by Janusz Anderman encapsulates a symptomatic episode. During an aimless stroll, two young writers discuss literature, or rather, attempt to have a discussion. They have difficulty in formulating any viewpoint. The reason is twofold. The incident takes place in the days of martial law, when, following the unexpected turn of political events and the unprecedented situation in which Polish society then found itself, even to think about writing seemed devoid of any sense. As one of the young men complains, "Everything that has been so far is now a thing of the past." The two are also hamstrung by the presence of their "guardian angel", a secret policeman who shadows their every step and eavesdrops on their every word.

There is nothing in this scene that transcends the canon of realistic description, yet at the same time it is vested with a symbolic dimension. It may be seen as a stark image or metaphor epitomizing the quintessential features of the situation in which Polish literature found itself after December 1981, when the dictatorship of party, policy and army declared war on the nation. Viewed from one angle, the situation was new and unexpected, and it imposed on literature the fundamental and formidable task of interpreting and perpetuating in words the experiences that had altered the collective awareness of society no less than the conceptual world of each individual member of that society. On the other hand, as is often the case in totalitarian states, literature — being by the very nature of things suspected of nonconformity — stood before an elemental danger: it no longer had to fight for freedom of expression alone, but for its very survival.

After December 1981, new forms of police control over culture supplemented the restrictions of censorship that had been in force for decades, ever since the system of prior censorship was introduced at the time of the birth of People(s Poland. It was no accident that some of Poland(s most interesting writers were to be found among the thousands of internees rounded up in the first days of martial law. It was no mere chance that the Union of Polish Writers, the professional organization that provided help and support for writers, was first suspended, then — in the summer of 1983 — dissolved and replaced by a puppet organization of the same name that was totally subordinated to the authorities and is to this day boycotted by almost all writers of standing. And it was more than just a coincidence that police raids, arrests and draconian court sentences rained with particular relentlessness on those who produce and circulate independent literature: underground publishers, printers and distributors. It is thanks to their combined efforts that, despite persecution and confiscation, several hundred uncensored periodicals and hundreds of uncensored books are still circulating in Poland today.

One of the paradoxes of totalitarian states is that their literature, whilst forced to fend off the deadly threat from the power apparatus, is at the same time summoned to life by society(s strong need to hear the truth about its own fate. Such are the circumstances in Poland today. The major turning point in the consciousness of Polish society that came about at the beginning of the eighties thanks to Solidarity derived, *inter alia*, from the widespread realization of the need for freedom of expression. And practical conclusions were also drawn on a massive scale. Undermined from the mid-seventies onward by the individual initiatives of underground publishers, the supremacy of censorship was openly challenged in the Solidarity period by the network of independent publishing houses, distribution points and even libraries that in a short time spread throughout the country. The new consumers took avidly to the uncensored publications, whether of *belles-lettres*, history, current political writing or investigative journalism. Readers fed for so many years on a barren diet of censored books and censored news hungered not only for straightforward information about facts hitherto concealed, but craved an authentic artistic expression of their own experiences and ordeals. The demand grew in the grim months of martial law, disproving the old saw about the Muses being silent when the thunderous cannon roar; and this hunger has shown no signs of abating.

Over the last few years Polish literature has thus had to face a peculiar duality, poised as it is between the overt hostility of state and the inordinate expectations of society that require a writer to perform exceptionally onerous duties. The basic difficulty here is to reconcile two conflicting demands. To remain faithful to his own vocation, the writer must at the same time voice the aspirations of the public at large and the aspirations of the individual "I". By their very nature the two do not always coincide.

Janusz Anderman ranks among those Polish writers who have succeeded in finding an artistically convincing solution to the dilemma. His prose satisfies to an amazing degree the demand for a realistic picture of present-day Poland, whilst at the same time it remains an expression of the author's individualistic stance. Anderman's achievement is all the more noteworthy in that "post-war" literature — that is to say, literature written after 1981 — has scored most of its successes in the realm of lyric poetry, which by its nature reacts more promptly to emotional upheavals and social revaluations.

Anderman's literary development to date leads in sequence to the artistic solutions that characterize his latest stories. In many respects his biography is typical for a whole generation of writers now in their late thirties, who were born and bred in People's Poland. Born in 1949, he studied Slavonic Literatures at the Jagiellonian University in Krakow. After taking his degree he worked for a short time as a reporter on the periodical *Student* (The Student), a bimonthly whose heyday was the early seventies. The authorities, however, soon identified it as being overly independent, and it was subjected to increased censorship. Anderman was unable to find his place in the newly doctored *Student*. In 1976 he became involved with the underground publishing movement which was still in its infancy. Since 1978 he has been co-editor of *PULS*, one of the first uncensored literary periodicals to have appeared in Poland. His first two books, *Zabawa w* gluchy telefon (Dead Telephone Games, 1976) and *Gra na zwloke* (Temporizing, 1979), were brought out by state publishing houses. But his next work, the present collection of stories, was uncensorable. In 1983 the Polish original was issued simultaneously by an emigré publisher in London and an underground printing house in Poland. From 1980 onward Anderman was actively involved in liaison work between the Union of Polish Writers and Solidarity. When martial law was declared he became a co-founder of the Committee of Aid for Internees, only to be arrested shortly afterwards himself and taken to the notorious Bialoleka jail, where he spent six months. After being released he travelled for a time in Western Europe, but subsequently returned to Poland, where he is living at present.

The literary generation to which Anderman belongs grew to maturity on such traumatic experiences as the student protests of 1968, the workers' riots of 1970 and 1976, the birth of an intellectual opposition in the seventies, followed by the creation of Solidarity in 1980 and the pacification of the country by the military regime in 1981. The "Generation of '68", as it is known, yielded a rich crop of poets in the main. Its poetry and its poetic programs have contributed to one of the most dramatic areas of change in modern Polish literature. Parallel to this revitalisation and revival of poetry, interesting changes have likewise taken place in the prose of the generation, though they are numerically fewer and of an admittedly narrower scope. The movement was, however, of sufficient importance for critics in the mid-seventies (perhaps somewhat overstating their case) to have called it a "revolution of young prose".

From the moment his first novel was published,

Anderman was to play a prominent role in this mini-revolution. His own artistic individuality and innovation derive from his skilful manipulation and combination of two seemingly conflicting perspectives: a "lyrical" individual point of view with ensuing looseness of novelistic structure, and a reflection of reality that is realistic in the extreme, one might even say naturalistic.

The realism of dialogues in Anderman's novels and stories in particular bears an absolute stamp, and one can safely claim that, with the possible exception of Miron Bialoszewski, an extraordinary poet of the spoken language, no Polish writer before Anderman has produced heroes speaking a language so close to the authentic speech of ordinary people. This aspect of Anderman's writing is particularly difficult to preserve in translation, and the English reader should bear in mind that the dialogues in the original Polish note with the fidelity of a tape recording the language used by the man in the street today, with all its idiosyncracies, phonetic to stylistic.

There is something more to this than literary technique or perfect authorial pitch. Like so many of the poets of his generation, Anderman sees colloquial speech as the reflection of social consciousness, in which "folk" spontaneity combines with the distorting influences of propaganda, and concreteness and bluntness enter into peculiar marriages with the colourless bureaucratese of newspapers and television.

Anderman's dialogue technique has proved to be a particularly handy device in the stories and vignettes that depict life under martial law. It is the reality of a brutal turning point in social consciousness, a grotesquely tragic catastrophe of delusions and hopes, the reality of a historical moment in which the human collectivity stands unexpectedly before an inexorable wall of falsehood and force. These stories were originally published under the Polish title *Brak tchu* (Breathless) — and a genuine sense of suffocation is the common experience of characters and readers alike. Anderman spares no one, comforts no one, creates no new optimistic delusions, leaves little room for hope. Hope here survives only "behind the high prison walls" where political detainees are serving their sentences. Ordinary citizens — those tired and humiliated people who "in the wink of an eye have learned to assume the stance of the condemned" — are bereft of it. But for the writer hope can manifest itself in the very resilience of the human mind, preserved against all odds in the abused, maltreated language of everyday life. Even the most alien, repellent and despairing reality becomes a human reality if the intellect can find a name for it. And "names" can range from complex literary works to the most rudimentary statements, such as the signboard announcing after the dispersal of a demonstration by tear gas, "Shop closed on account of gas". Face to face with hopelessness Anderman finds the only solution within a writer's reach, the only solution worthy of a writer: hopelessness must first be called by name. The problem of what is to happen next begins outside literature.

Stanislaw Baranczak
Harvard University
August 1985

POLAND
UNDER BLACK LIGHT

Freeze-frame One

…The country is fading on the maps, bit by bit withering away; the outlines of the borders blur, soften, spread out in all three directions of the world, so it becomes impossible for sensitive fingertips to feel them any more; his town disintegrated and can be found only in the dull scraps of his memory.

The streets end unexpectedly in army barricades; the tree, despite the proclamation of spring, is dry, leafless, the house on Przechodnia Street is deserted.

The addresses in the notebook go blank or crumple away; life according to the rules remains; behind the high prison walls — only there does hope survive.

Barbed air wounds the lungs, people forget the future, their world has the short life of film clips, notes lost on scattered cards.

The town is gasping for breath, and a woman in a washed-out smock getting out of the official black Volga on the main road looks desperately around, unable to remember where she was supposed to deliver the bowl of soup she carries on a plastic tray…

— Sipping tea is one thing, but this is something else — the soldier growls, emphatically adjusting his machine gun…

Sinking Wells

I stood by the pump. Dug in firmly with my feet. My left leg thrust back, rooted in a clump of dried grass. The right one flexed at the knee, freer, so that it did not have to bear my weight. The left leg did that job without so much as a tremor.

I looked ahead; there were braided knots of veins bulging on the backs of my hands. Branching off in every direction, they wrapped the entire hand in a loving gesture and disappeared only at the fingers, where they ran more deeply. They proved the importance of hands, they were their own confirmation. There was an uneasy stir and pulsing beneath the skin and the strain caused bright spots to appear at the wrists. Fingers, wrists, shoulders, the hands were tired. They felt today's work and that of previous days. They felt every minute.

The meadow was still ablaze in the heat; without a breath of wind the dry grass moved like green tongues of fire.

…well, so they covered my face with a mask, I couldn't speak, 'cos I mean I had my face covered, I just motioned with my head to show I was suffocating, when they told me to take a deep breath I felt I was suffocating, I motioned with my head and it all went blank;

suddenly they woke me up and then I was surprised I couldn't fall asleep, tell me, and the operation was over; I didn't even know when I'd dropped off, 'cos when they put that mask over my face I couldn't utter a word, you see I had my face covered, only I motioned with my head to show I was suffocating, when they told me to breathe deep I felt I was suffocating, I motioned with my head and it all went blank; so when I woke up...

— P-pull, cuntie — the voice seemed to come from under the earth. My fingers tightened their grip on the warm iron of the winch.

— It's running, cuntie — I turned more slowly, more rhythmically. The tin bucket loaded with sand sailed out above the last ring. Holding the winch in my right hand, I leaned over to the left and pulled the bucket away in the direction of the mound of earth. There I tipped out the load; the sand was moist, and a pool of muddy water had gathered at the bottom of the bucket.

— It's running onto me, cuntie. We'll have to use the hood — came a shuffling and scraping out of the dark. Then he appeared. He supported his shoulders and legs against the rings and, twisting about like a worm, worked his way up through the well-shaft towards the torrid daylight.

— One day you'll have a fall, Mr. Oblegorek — I said.

— If I'd wanted to fall I'd have killed myself a hundred times already. Think I'm fool enough for that? We'll have to use the hood, seeing as you're pouring mud over me head.

— Sorry.

— Sorry, sorry. When we was building a road once with me brother-in-law Wysocki it was sorry sir sorry sir all the time. There was five of us lads and so — please sir, thank you sir, and whenever one pulled out a pack of Sport fags Do have one of mine, oh no really do try one of mine. Well so we was breaking up stone and one of 'em hammered me brother-in-law Wysocki's finger instead, and he said look where you're 'itting, you son-of-a-bitch, and that was the end of the please sirs. So just you stop apologizing, we'll use the hood.

He sat down on a small mound of moist sand that had been freshly excavated from inside the hot earth, pulled off his boots and squeezed out his foot-cloths. He set his short-helved shovel aside on the grass for it to dry out.

— Never leave the shovel at the bottom. See what I mean, the rust gets it. But a boot's a boot. You're safe in your boots. Now bare hands is different. I was cutting chaff once and stuck me finger in. One blow and it was a gonner. I yelled for the old woman whose chaff I was cutting; I says, see if there ain't a finger in that chaff. Well and so there is, she says. I pressed it on, and tied it up in a rag and thinks, if it works it works, if it don't it don't. Agony I might say. In the morning I went to the lady doc, she undid the bandage and examined it, all right then, if it heals it heals, if it don't it don't. Then she smeared it with some yellow muck. And I've still got it. That finger there. It's not much good at bending, but it can still lift a table. Just the thing for well-sinking. Anyway I was a born well-sinker, cuntie. Didn't grow on purpose, see.

...the red vocalist sings a Parisian tango, the crowd moves in rhythm, ominously; a woman in a white cap and pompom; sweat streams down her, her buttocks wrapped in elastic trousers; a little man in a red lace

4

shirt nestles his face between the woman's breasts and shuffles at her side, and she holds on to his sideburns...

I propped myself against the well-casing, as it gave off some coolness and shade for my shoulders. But not much, and it no longer nursed my legs. We hadn't been sitting for long, and the shadow still hadn't budged.

— Mister Oblegorek, that well could be a sundial.

— What you mean?

— Only you'd have to sink the rings aslant. At an angle.

— A slanting well? Must be the heat today that makes you talk such rubbish. Let's get on. It's a decent enough job, only the day's too long.

— The day's not that bad. It's bearable.

...when we took the old fruit we all stood round her, she was on the trolley on the way to the operating theatre and basically she was gone, she just held out a hand and mumbled; I'd like to go on a train journey, a long long way just for fun, I'd like to take a train; we were all waiting and thinking she was dead or whatever, when they brought her up at last, eyes shut, so we all touched her, still warm, therefore alive, and so on right through the night; the operation, when they put that mask on my face I felt I was suffocating and I motioned with my head because my face was covered...

— It's the night that's too long, Mister Oblegorek.

— In the night you sleep with a woman. Or you run round begging with your prick. Let's get on. When a bloke earns a bit of money it does something for his spirits. And the bitch wouldn't give a hundred-zloty note for a good building job. She said no, she'd have none of it. I wanted to take her twenty years back, but she wouldn't look at me. I hadn't a bean. See, and now she's buried her old man, and I'll not be having her now. But in those days I was running after her like a mad dog. She was, you might say, badly dispositioned towards my person. Now I'm the artful one these days. If I wasn't, I wouldn't be sporting a nylon raincoat. But in those days I was like a mad dog. Like I always had her before my eyes. A strapping woman she was. Today she's just a runt. And she wouldn't give a hundred-zloty note for a good job. Once me brother-in-law Wysocki and me was building a barn. We had a carpenter with us, and me brother-in-law's a decent fellow 'cos he knows how to drink. Cuntie, we went and asked the farm-lady for a hundred-zloty note to brick up in a corner for good luck and what have you. Cuntie, she didn't want to at first, but she did in the end. We stuck that hundred-note in the foundation, gave it a splash of cement, and when the woman went off, cuntie, we whipped the bank note out again and sent the lad for some wine. He brought five bottles and there was enough change for sixty cigs — just fifty groszy short. Then the carpenter paid for another round, we knocked it all back. And it went on like that for six days. The carpenter took an advance of a thousand zlotys and we carried on drinking, then he packed up and went, because Sunday came, and so we never saw him again.

I stood by the pump. Dug in firmly with my feet. My left leg thrust back, rooted in a clump of dried grass. The right one flexed at the knee, freer, so that it did not have to bear my weight. The left leg did that job without so much as a tremor.

I was watching the winch. Not the vast small world behind my back. An ugly world where Sunday is like a stain of mildew.

...what's to drink; why tell you, you always order the same, there's beer; someone says, what a thought, one could say that those trees die standing; I don't want to be a snob by which I mean to follow public opinion, but there are two camps, one against, and that is contra, the other for, and that means for; please sir, a beer, I'm feeling low, if you've finished your food kindly vacate your place; people distort and exaggerate; I run a sulfur mag and when I want to go somewhere I just say that I'm going and I go, I write about foremen and the like, just for reading the papers I've got more cash in hand than you; please sir, but do tell me, are you a prince or aren't you, only please tell me, my dear; I'm from pretty good stock; but are you a prince, mate, or aren't you...

The landscape passes by along the train. The day breaks out, then subsides and holds steady. Oblegorek introduces me with a shout:

— Grandpa, I've found a helper. He thumbed a ride out here.

— So put it under the pear tree then — he replies.

And the next day I was sitting in the pine trees against the sun and I could see Oblegorek's shadow. He walked round the meadow on his wide-apart legs, and stretched his hands out before him like a blind man. He was holding a forked birch branch carved of that gentlest of trees and slowly he stumped forward. His white-brimmed well-sinker's hat was tilted back on his head. He was absorbed and tense, and the veins sprouted out on his temples like little brooks from under the brim.

— Jesus, Jesus — groaned the farm woman crouching behind me as, hard-handed, she blessed the hot air in four parts.

The heat was slumbering. The dried grass did not bind the earth together, and it now rose in clouds of dust from under the impatient stamping boots.

— May the Lord God cripple that motherfucker. May He strike him, the monster — growled the widow, tearing pieces of living flesh from the body of her neighbour who had barred the way to his well, that she now had to pay these thousands.

— May the plague take him, amen.

The birch withe twitched in Oblegorek's hands. Finally it curved down towards the parched earth, and he drew violently to a halt.

— I feel water here, this is where we'll bore.

— Jesus — groaned the widow.

— I feel water — he repeated and sat down on the edge of a hillock. He pulled out cigarettes, and the widow kept shaking her head wrapped in thoughts as heavy as the heat.

And then the first ring was lowered into the friable soil, and I had nothing to do. Oblegorek was fixing it, excavating as he went.

— Then you see me brother-in-law Wysocki, cuntie, was sinking a well. I only came to do the explosives, 'cos his son worked in the stone-pit and took as much dyno as he fancied. We dug out thirty metres in the rock, there was no water, but I thought, cuntie, hope no one falls in 'cos brother-in-law stinted on the timbering. Well, and it was brother-in-law Wysocki who fell in. I come running along, cuntie, and asks how he fell. On his head they said. So I says to me brother-in-law's son, better earth it over, you'll save on the funeral, besides it'ud be a sin to drink from the well now. No question of that he says, not at all, cuntie, must bring him up.

We sent one man down, because me brother-in-law's son didn't want to go down there himself, no way. But how to fish him out? They tie him under the armpits, then up shoot the arms, cuntie, and out he slips. Well then, I suggest tying him by the head, but then I thinks when the persecutor comes along he'll say we hung him. So we roped up his leg, I pulled, but the blood gushed out of him again, and the fellow at the bottom shouted that he's swamped in blood. And brother-in-law Wysocki's a decent bloke, 'cos he's a good drunk. He knew how to get drunk alright. And so thirty metres was wasted.

Oblegorek was standing in the first ring. It was not deep, so his head in the well-sinker's hat stuck out over the edge. And then it began to recede into the cavity, vanished altogether, and I stood with my left leg supporting and turned the warm metal of the winch. I looked in front of me. At the blazing meadow and above it.

Oblegorek is drilling in the soil; he digs stubbornly, and when I lean over the ring of darkness I cannot even see him. I only hear his voice, which seems to come from under the earth.

— She didn't want me, cuntie, so now she's buried her old man. And I was after her like a dog after a bitch, with my prick a-begging.

He drilled and penetrated deep, and up above I took the load, a bucketful of moist shavings. When the ring drew level with the surface, Oblegorek emerged from the darkness; he unhitched the bucket, placed one leg in the cable-loop, leaned the other leg and then his shoulder against the wall. I gave one turn of the winch, he sought support higher up, then the next turn and the next support, until he appeared in the sun. We fixed

9

the next ring. Oblegorek did not stop to rest. He did not even sit with a fag and smoke it out with his usual sense of purpose. He did not squeeze the water out of his foot-cloths, only went back into the darkness and drilled. In a passion for this living soil.

— And I was after her like a cur after a bitch. With my prick a-begging.

I looked in front of me. At the blazing meadow and above it. Towards the blue strip of pines and on the left towards a stand of young birches, the loveliest of trees, covered in bark warm as the skin on animal bellies. We looked for water, drilling to the source. My gaze did not reach beyond the blue strip of pines. They were the horizon. And those gentle birches.

No words could attack here. I was shielded by the calm of the meadow. Couldn't hear the barman standing with the shocked face, his torso cut in two by the metal tabletop.

...Jeez...Jeez, it's you, but I had a scare, they said you'd been killed in a crash, the car a write-off, but maybe they weren't talking about you, I can't remember now, jeez...I thought to myself, such a highbrow type, I thought to myself at once, as soon as I ever saw you here, it was a load of codswallop; do you know Lieutenant Smyk, wha', I'm buying a whole bottle, wha', I was doing the boilers for a certain professor and he tells me to do one and I did, do you know Lieutenant Smyk? I'll take a whole bottle; he stumbles over and like Christ falls spreadeagled on the wet tiles of the bog; the waitress swipes the client across his face, you've been asleep long enough, you know me madam from an honest day's work, and I know you from a dishonest one; what's that, the restaurant's about to close, the whores'll be round; I can tell you everything about yourself, mister, I'm a fortune-teller, a sort of clairvoyant, by the by, throw us some coppers for a beer...

Pray that they never drag me stoned from a taxi. That I never hold a nosegay in my hands and stammer, long live, long live. That a frightened taxi driver never mutters who's going to pay for the puke, who's going to pay for cleaning up the puke...

The maidenly skin of the gentle birches on the horizon. And the dark blue splash of pines.

— Found it. There's a source, cuntie... — cried Oblegorek twisting his way from one ring to the next towards the light. His trousers were wet above his boots.

— Found it. When you look at the sky from below you can see stars in broad daylight. I'm stunned, cuntie. Last time I saw stars from a well.

We extracted the first bucket. The water was yellow and muddy. Opaque.

— We'll have to pull lots of muck out before it's clear — Oblegorek said reflectively as we sat by the scrubbed table of white planks.

— I'm so glad you've come, I was beginning to think you'd got lost — Grandpa fretted about the parlour, spreading his arms like a grey moth knocking against the walls. — *The Courier*, do you think it's a good paper?

There was a bottle on the table.

— It doesn't stink of rotgut. Grandpa distilled it three times.

— Have some cold meat — he pushed the black pudding, looking like caviar, in my direction. There was bread, mustard, tea. Everything was there. The white planks of the freshly scrubbed table.

— It popped out small and hairy, half-pig, half-goat, half-man — Grandpa mumbled. — That's the child she produced. It was in the *Courier*. Is the lemon good?

— And how... — Oblegorek was opening a second bottle and was hunched over the table.

— Now that's what I'd — he moved up closer. He jerked his head back, then splashed the rest onto the floor and put the glass aside — The widow lives near here. We could travel a long way to sink another well, but we don't have to. Know what we'll do? We'll chuck a dead cat down her well. Then it'll have to be earthed over for fear of the plague. I've got just the carcass. And we'll drill another well for her nearby. I've got just the carcass. We'll throw it down her well. Only first, we've got to choose a muddy one and only when it comes up clear...

I filled my glass, knocked it back and threw the rest onto the floor. I pushed my glass aside and lit a cigarette.

— And we'll sink another well. Why travel far when there's work at hand. I've got just the carcass and we'll dig...

— I shan't be able to sink any more wells — I said with a laugh. — Must be going.

— What? Didn't I pay you enough? I thought we'd hit it off...

— It's not that. You pay good money.

— Then what's the bother?

— No bother. I hadn't told you but I must be off. You'll have to look for water with someone else. That's life.

— What? Did you hear, Grandpa? Leaving us, he is.

— So put it under the pear tree then — he replied.

1973

Freeze-frame Two

...That December day they wanted to put flowers by the shipyard gate, in memory of their dead of eleven years ago, but armoured cordons stopped them, and they could see the approaching buses only from a distance above the domes of helmets; they saw people getting off and bustling cameramen; they observed those people laying elaborate wreaths of artificial flowers for their own victims.

That first day, the television newscasters could be differentiated from the audience by their tight-fitting uniforms; the notes they held low in their fingers and glanced at made them talk mechanically; the words rolled in the white glow of the spotlights, long wrinkles on their foreheads; there were people among us who consciously sought to cause unrest, so that Polish blood would be spilled. One day history will sentence them harshly and severely for sowing discord, obstinacy, irresponsibility, lack of imagination. Their consciences will be stained by Polish blood. They should be made to face the mothers of the killed Wujek miners,* in the name of what cause did they push for confrontation? They ought to be made to look into the eyes of the victims' mothers.

— Let us bow our heads before these unnecessary deaths — the talking notes rattle, the heads of the newscasters lowered as if fearing a sudden blow.

In the room next to the television studio, the book-keeper fills in the last lines of the wage-list.

That first night, the overcrowded prisons did not sleep, nor did a host of army sentinels...

*Wujek Mine — seven miners died resisting martial law in December 1981.

13

Night Shift in Emergency

Down the airless tunnel of the hospital corridor a trolley moved silently on rubber wheels. On it a man lay pinned down by the sinewy hands of the ward attendants, struggling to raise himself, shouting into the closed space, spare me, you butchers, bleed your guts out, have mercy!

His head, suddenly quiet, dropped back on the stained oil-cloth; he pulled it strenuously away from under the strong fingers of the women and continued his pleading in a scream that bounced off the walls of the corridor like sparks.

The doors of the elevator slammed and the voice was trapped in the shaft, its gloom dispersed by the husky laughter of the operator; with one hand he worked the lever, while the other wandered towards the ward attendant's crotch, shielded by her grey rag of a uniform.

A young doctor rushed into the ward and glanced round rapaciously as if counting his inventory; there were not many patients yet and he eyed the recumbent figures with an air of reproach, as though they had let him down. His gaze wore the conviction that one clean stroke of the scalpel can alter a man's life.

He circulated along the narrow passages between the beds, taking a close look at the patients before their long journey to the operating theatre.

With a razor in her slender fingers a nurse went up to the inert and flabby body of a man, could you please shave for the operation.

— So long as I don't nick myself — the man whispered, his forehead flecked with drops of sweat. He slowly twisted over onto his side, peeled down his pyjama bottoms and guided the blade over his belly. His skin sounded like torn parchment. Two convalescents, recovered since the last shift, were playing pontoon, while keeping a close eye on the world around them. A youngster lay on the bed next to them; there was no sign of suffering in his eyes, which were covered by spongy, loaf-like swellings.

— You, balloon-head, two more have already croaked it in that shirt of yours. It's got two seams. That means it's been split open twice on a stiff. Pontoon — he cried, after a glance at his cards.

The boy raised his head, but could not see his shirt, so he simply fingered the two seams which stretched from his neck down towards his belly.

The first patient to have been operated on during that shift was wheeled into the ward. As in some ritual, the nurses stretched the body onto the bed and meticulously covered the feet with the pillow they had removed from beneath the resting head. The bulb of the drip-feed swayed above the bedding, filtering light over the patient's motionless hands.

— Don't sleep, don't sleep, how do you feel...

He dwelt on the question at length, how do I feel, how do I feel.

— I'm dead.

The young doctor ushered in the next trolley in procession. Lay the old boy on this one — Hey, grandad, so we meet again, how about chopping off the other leg?

— Give him a good look over, then get him out and onto the operating table.

A nurse confusedly wrapped the thin body in the tentacle wires that joined it to the electrocardiogram.

— How can I connect you when you haven't got a leg? How can I connect you?

— But I can feel my leg. I can still feel it. My leg.

He turned his head towards the pillow of the bed next door, what're you here for, I've been around these hospitals you know.

His neighbour listened avidly, joy mounting in his torpid eyes.

— Pretty sickness you've got there. I had me leg off here not long ago. It's a decent place, real OK. I waited a whole week for the emergency ward. Just to get back here. This time I'm in for cancer. That's how it is. Just as I get used to life without a leg, have a few drinks, manage not to care any more. I've done my bit of boozing and dancing after all. It's been twelve days now I've gone without food, so a bloke begins to feel run down.

The young doctor chivvied the nurse, who was awkwardly plucking out the hairs on the old man's belly.

— Leave his prick, can't you? Finish prepping him and get him down to the theatre.

The convalescents tore their eyes away from their cards, while you're at it, nurse, give him something to remember in heaven. The girl's face was in flames and her fingers instinctively clutched the uniform which was half-open above her breasts.

A yellow stain the shape of Asia spread on the patient's bedcover. His hands had dropped, dragged down by the weight of the urine-bottle.

After a couple of hours the old man's bed is occupied again, and another mouth emerges from under the dressings like a flower, complaining to the radiator.

— Oh Jesus, oh jesu, ojesu, ojes, ojee.

— Sister. What's happened to the old boy. His bed's been taken.

— Wa'. Gone to another ward.

A solitary shoe, discarded memory of a leg, protrudes from under the bed.

The Gipsy dropped dead tonight, says the ward attendant, and burst out laughing.

— His missis brought 'im a chicken. Must have nicked it from some hen-coop. And he bunged it under his blanket. Ate the whole bloody thing. He pegged out on the spot. Well, I mean really. The second day after his op. Fairly stuffed himself he did.

An old man presses twenty zlotys into her hungry palm; treat yourself, go on. And could I have the bed pan, begging your pardon, Miss?

Coiled in a blue dressing-gown I stand in the corridor peering through the glazed doors at the young doctor who has just performed an operation, who now smokes a cigarette and talks to the nurse in the duty-room. He leans his palm against the wall above her head, and the girl hugs herself with her arms, emphasizing for his benefit the breasts under her overalls.

The young doctor notices me, well now then, are you going to sign the consent form?

— No. Don't you count on it.

— Now try a rational approach. Really it's only a minor operation. You'll be good as new. Decide now while I'm asking politely.

— Out of the question.

The thin scalpel reflects bright outside the window. In the street the engine of the night bus rumbles.

Two ticket collectors can be seen dragging a man out of the bus. He resists. They twist his arms and drag him under the street-lamp which struggles to emit some light.

I return to the ward and pass by the bursting drip-feeds. A student nurse puts a chair by the old man's bed.

She sits down, wraps herself in her grey cape and delicately unfolds the membrane of a newspaper.

— Nurse, do you know the joke about the guy who went to hospital with a dislocated prick? — the convalescents ask, setting their cards aside.

They gaze at her with lustful eyes. With a fixed unflinching stare they carve her up between them, each grabbing his share. Tomorrow they'll no longer stack the cards in equal parts.

The girl bows her head over the film listings. Her hair smothers her face and covers the blush in her cheeks like powder.

— And have you heard the one about the monk's hood? Like to hear it?

— Is it saucy? — she shyly ventures.

— You like them spicy. Don't kid me...A lull descends on the ward.

— It's the two from the other ward — the attendants whisper.

Outside the window the town flickers before daybreak; the houses tremble slightly, the last women from the station close up like prayer books.

Workers crawl to their factories, whose chimneys have swallowed a mouthful of rainwater.

At dawn a pretty nurse comes running into the ward.

— Pee, pee, why haven't you peed for the samples yet? Quick now!

The young doctor ends his shift and will soon be back in his office, sifting out patients. He is out of his white uniform. Over his shoulders he wears a suede jacket, warm as a moist hand.

— Why aren't you sleeping?

— Why do you ask?

— Well, what about the operation? Just for interest's sake.

— There's not going to be any operation.

— You'll end up badly then. In a couple of days you'll be singing a different tune.

— Don't be ridiculous.

The young doctor jerks out his left leg, his palm clenches hedgehog-like into a fist which he lands in the pit of my stomach.

I bend as if bowing in thanks; my mouth fails to inhale.

The young doctor runs down the steps and out of the hospital.

Once in the street he glances back up at the window and sees me. Then he slams his car door and roars off into town.

Unbandaged for dressing, the patient's head wakes up like a hard day.

Hands flounder towards the empty strawberry jam jars. Cards with surnames written in rounded, girlish lettering are stuck on them.

Moans rise in the ward. In the changing-room the nurses pare skin-tight white overalls from their bodies, scanning one another with jealous glances.

— The one with the big tits is on duty today — says

the convalescent.

— The one with 'em bursting right out of her uniform. Sister, how many have snuffed it in emergency to date?

— What? What's today? — the old man comes out of his drugged sleep. A day beggaring description begins.

1975

Freeze-frame Three

...These women who age and go grey in a few months...

These women who move skilfully through the tunnels of clothes, tins, packets and medicines which fill the glazed corridors of the monastery...

These women who perch like grey sparrows on the cartons to snatch a quick rest, who do not even think about the night.

They are making parcels for those known only by their surnames and for the orphaned families. They sit on the boxes, and the stone floor swells their voices to infinity.

— In one of the camps, the screws were beating people and ordering them to kiss their boots.

— In another, a woman has been told that her son died, but they will let her attend the funeral only if she signs the declaration of loyalty.

— A man is in hiding, so they keep coming to his mother asking where he is, and she says she has no idea, so they threaten to take her to the mortuary every Monday to look at the new bodies, just in case her son's is among them.

— When they were taking a couple, they put their children into a police orphanage; they told them they would never get their children back.

— He is in prison, and she is alone with the child, who is just beginning to talk; but she is deaf and dumb, and the child can only repeat her mumbling; so what can it learn from her, it just repeats her sounds, nothing more.

— They confiscated the medicine of a woman prisoner who was sick, and when she complained, told her they could give her rope to hang herself any time.

— One mother who works in the secret police denounced her own son; just now I made a parcel for him. The women stop, but the sound of their voices hovers in the silence.

— Have you heard this one? The ZOMO Special Forces policeman goes to the doctor with a crowbar in his back. Mother-in-law? asks the doctor. No, says he, "the Uncle" (Wujek)...Mine...

The women walk away through the labyrinth, paper rustles; don't forget, take off those coloured Western wrappers, they drive the wardens mad...

Turkish Baths

The plaster is covered in small crevices left over from a bout of black smallpox some thirty years back.

With its remaining strength a crooked showcase — the lacquer cracked like lichens — hangs by one hook on the wall. Behind the misty pane three drawings by children are visible, above there's an inscription: Always United, first, second, third prize. Reach for the stars. In each picture the Kremlin is painted in splashes and splotches of water-colour. Out of each Kremlin, from the highest tower, a steel sputnik rears up with the air of a vicious spermatazoon that would spring an unwanted pregnancy on the world.

This is the entrance to the Turkish baths; behind it, however, could be almost any institution.

It may be that the door whose station-coloured paint is quietly peeling leads to the baths.

It may be that inside there are low corridors, slippery balustrades sweating with steam which no one touches for fear of leaving fingerprints, stairs, heavy curtains and upright tin ashtrays. An oppressive smell of damp linen and, surely, a little woman selling admission tickets, a woman with a huge head tilting backward.

Narrow passages lead in different directions, baths,

needle baths, showers, mud-baths; enamel plates with effaced inscriptions hang on the doors.

People cling to wooden benches, waiting for someone to restore their urge to live. Their eyes show deep trust as though they were preparing for confession.

Every now and again some attendants appear swathed in grey overalls and, keen-eyed, fish their customer out of the crowd.

A huge sheet bruised all over by rubber stamps divides the steam bath from a room where there is a buffet with a small table and a solitary chair, on which someone is sitting. Other figures, wrapped in lengths of towelling stand about in motionless poses, like monuments of the times, surrounded by filaments of steam as silent as first snow.

The buffet attendant's head moves behind a high counter, looking as though it is sliding along the top, which is greased with moisture. The buffet attendant clatters the bottles of Grodzisko beer. He greedily raises the bottles to his mouth as though he would like to drink from each in turn. He has a large gap between his front teeth into which he wedges the tip of the bottle-top, then jerks it from the neck at one go. He has no time to wipe away the whisks of foam that escape. The foam settles on his mouth, so that the head bobbing along the counter looks like a madman's.

He hands out the bottles, which are received in silence, tosses the coins into an old ivory plastic floor polish box, rattles the coins, then laughs at some point in space.

— Everything's fine. Halva, pumice, rubbing oil.

— All we need is whores for a knobbing — the man at the table replies. — Then we'd all be cock of the walk.

— Yes, then, halva, pumice and rubbing oil — the buffet attendant laughs through his foam-flecked lips.

— Boss. Has a dark fellow with close-cropped hair asked for me today? — the man at the table inquires.

— Not yet he hasn't — the buffet attendant gurgles. If he was supposed to come, he'll come. Mr. Wladzio came asking, but he left.

— More's the pity. There's no fun without Mr. Wladzio. When he tells a joke, waves his prick...

— Halva, pumice and rubbing oil — roars the buffet attendant, and he wipes the tears streaming down his face on the banknote portrait of Warynski.

— Anyone got a hundred? 'Cos I'm fresh out of cash. Could do with a drink — the man at the table pushes the bottle aside.

The dumb figures in white shake their heads.

The curtain separating the room from the Turkish bath moves imperceptibly; a figure appears cautiously from behind it and, hugging the wall, flits past furtively towards the buffet.

— Hi, Attaché. How're ya.

Attaché stops abruptly in mid-step and places his bare foot warily on the tiling, as if he were testing the ground.

— H-hello.

— Let's get cracking — the man at the table winks to the dumb figures. He raises himself an inch and extracts from under his seat a book in frail, insecure covers.

— Attaché. Like to do a spot of business?

— I-I-I sh-should s-s-ay.

— Attaché. See this tome here. It's dramas. You'll net two hundred. You can have it for one, then pop down to the second-hand shop and dispose of it for two.

— I-i-i-is it w-wor-worth it?

— I should think so. It's a rarity. Listen, Attaché. Valentyn Zielencov comes under the influence of his master Vaverlejski's Western life style. He gives priority to private affairs, and neglects production and cultural work in the theatrical ensemble attached to the factory. It is only the decisive attitude of his comrades and the educational activities of the corporate team that enable both Kostya and Valentyn to adopt a positive attitude to problems. Characteristically, all the plays have an optimistic ending, showing further evolutionary perspectives for supporters of the struggle for peace and socialism. In keeping with the historical development of humanity, the vanquished are representatives of the depraved and rotting capitalist world. The victors are splendid, high-minded people who are fighting to achieve, or have already achieved, the system of justice and happiness, communism. You can see how good the introduction is already. It's called Friends of Art. One hundred for that is an absolute gift. I wouldn't swindle you, Attaché, now would I? Would I?

— Wai-wai-wait a mo — Attaché feverishly replies, then dashes behind the curtain.

— You can open some bottles, Boss.

The buffet attendant's head glides towards a crate of bottles; he picks up several at a time like a bouquet in his two stubby hands, and the badly stuck-on labels swirl towards the floor like dried leaves.

— We've got it made here, you and me, Boss, haven't we? You cook 'em, we peck 'em. Stylish. As for that lot — he points at the silent figures in white — they ought to fix red ties to their diapers. You shouldn't let people onto the premises without red ties.

26

— I'll say. Halva, pumice and rubbing oil. Yes or no?

The monuments in white raise their bottles to their mouths.

The curtain shudders, Attaché emerges as though he has been given a push from behind, and skulks towards the man at the table.

— Give the cash to the Boss — he nods towards the buffet attendant. Attaché halts abruptly in mid-step, then turns round and places the banknote gingerly on the counter. The buffet attendant instantly unsticks it from the moist surface.

— Take the opus — the man at the table says. Attaché grabs the book, then minces towards the curtain, but pauses again for a moment and looks imploringly at the buffet attendant.

— I-I-I say, Bo-oss, cou-ou-ouldn't I ha-a-ave a c-cou-couple of bottle-tops for the for the ch-ch-il-dren?

— Can't do it, ol' boy. As true as I live. I've also got to take something back to my little brood, you know.

— Ri-i-ight you-a-a-are — whispers Attaché, vanishing behind the curtain with the book under his arm.

The man at the table tilts his head backwards and allows the beer to flow freely. The monuments in white adjust their towels, padding their spongy bodies in them. The steam resounds softly in white.

The door slowly opens; the newcomer stops and scans the motionless figures for some familiar faces.

— You can't be admitted in civies — comes the voice of the buffet attendant.

— It's for me, Boss — the man at the table says. — I've got to fix the lad with a job. Hi-ya.

— Cheers.

— My buddy — the man at the table says, turning aside to the silent figures. — He was writing his Ph.D. and got kicked out at the last lap. He had the wrong sort of friends. Those types from KOR, know what I mean. Got involved in distributing those illegal rags. Now he's high and dry. *Mit Frau und Kinder*. Homeless. you ought'a help a fellow when he's high and dry, right? — he winks knowingly at his audience.

The upright figures are silent. The newcomer walks up to the table.

— Drinkie? — the seated figure asks.

— Why not.

— Boss, open us a couple of bottles. You pay the Boss, mate. Twelve a bottle.

The buffet attendant once again is foaming at the mouth, the falling bottle-tops and coins emit a delicate tinkle. The men in white drink silently.

— What sort of work are you after? — the man at the table asks.

— Well, I don't know what the prospects are...

— There are plenty of openings. For the time being you've got two options. Either the culture department at the municipal offices. Ideological work. Variety. Get me? Some sort of planning. Writing up charts and diagrams. Organizational stuff. Always something new. Or else a Scouts' broadcasting station. You can do a couple of programs for a try. Know how to use a tape recorder?

— Depends what sort.

— Outside the studio you normally take a Philips cassette. I reckon you know how to press a button. Rustle up a couple of programs, and they'll sign a contract with you. Say some sentence or other. Let's hear if you've got a broadcasting voice.

— What should I say?

— You've said it. Just what I wanted. That'll do. Your voice's OK. Now pop down to the delicatessen for a couple of bottles.

— What should I get?

— Hooch. Ordinary hooch. And something to follow. Anything will do. Piece of mortadella. Or Tshombe's ear. Or terrazzo. Anything. We must wet the deal.

— Right you are. I shan't be long. 'Cept there might be a line. But not necessarily. I'll soon be back. Things were looking bad. Couldn't find my footing. I'll be back right away. But it's sure? That job I mean?

— I should say so. Whatever did you think? So long as you like kids it's *pas de problème*. You can stop worrying.

The newcomer disappears behind the door. The silent figures in white remain motionless by their bottles.

The man sitting at the table licks a chrysanthemum of foam that has calmly blossomed on the bottleneck, pulls a cigarette out of the pack and turns towards the petrified head of the buffet attendant.

— Business is ticking over, eh? I've already knocked back a crate of hooch on that Scouts' radio station. There are more of those unemployed duffers every day. I love the Scouts for it. And you'll have your share by the by, Boss.

— I should say. Where did you net him?

— They're hanging about all over the place. He popped up in some boozer or other. You've got to put yourself in another man's shoes. Agreed?

— Halva, pumice and rubbing oil — the head of the buffet attendant laughs. And don't you throw away the beer labels. I'll take'em home. Must bring something for the kids, you know...

Speechless, the white-clad chorus waits.

Freeze-frame Four

...The wind is blowing scraps of newspaper along New World Street, the papers wipe mud off the asphalt; the patient newsprint absorbs insistent headlines like blood: production and productivity up, surplus of washing powder, economic ties with Angola expanded, Queen Marysia's quilt back in Wilanow, Polish youth active partner of the Party, White Lake white again, new activity at building sites, better and more in heavy industry, countrywomen's circles in action, communications not hit by crisis, genocide condemned, good start, new humane civilisation, softening of everyday hardship, ties of all cells strengthened, just what the people want; people are slipping along New World Street, reddish tears rolling from tightly closed lids, and on a door, a page from a school notebook, stuck on to the peeling paint with a Band-aid: Shop closed on account of gas...

Return Visit

As you get closer and closer to that ominous structure, each step you take will be twice as heavy, and that odious front will rise to meet you, will expand and will overshadow you.

And even if you pause for a moment's respite, you are coming ever closer to the place, coated in its grey protective rot of plaster that flakes onto the pavement.

With each reluctant step it looms nearer and larger, it will engulf you and crush you. And you will look round uneasily, watching out for familiar eyes, or rather, an unfamiliar face. You will peer superstitiously over your left shoulder, casting fearful glances this way and that; just hoping that no one will see you, as that gate of all gates swallows you.

Every step will catch in your throat, climb higher and higher, increasing the distance between you and that imagined refuge where you were so patently visible in your hiding.

You will come closer and closer to that dark building. This return visit is your reply to the callers who dropped by your place and left their card. You had given up expecting them; they were not interested that you might prefer another date or would even be happy to decline the invitation; it occurred to you then that you and they had nothing in common.

They could not entertain the thought of your letting them down; they were looking for you quite impatiently.

You will glance back again; no one can see you, and all you will see is the everyday view behind your back: rolling life, rolling tramcars, the two-dimensional picture of people on the downgrade, a picture full of dissonances, that no one will now succeed in clearing, or even try.

Passing through the gate, you will turn suddenly into the pale shadows. Humid decaying darkness will lick your face. You will be for sure the next in the procession and not the last to pay a return visit to one of these buildings. They spring up everywhere, swelling like blisters in every town, in central squares named more often than not after Liberty.

Though the button of the bell is mounted in the doorframe, you will knock on the grey wooden door; you will knock on that door which no canny bark-beetle would ever touch. You will wait an instant in silence, and then you will hear the jangle of invitation.

You will step inside and see a small corridor ending in another door mounted in a steel grating. You will see the opaque window shielding the duty-room and will set off in that direction, rummaging furiously meanwhile for your card. Emptying out your pockets.

In the duty-room, just behind the pane, you will notice an old table with its top covered in scratches, and a service cap perched at its edge. It looks for all the world as though the duty-officer's head is stuck inside it. From a distance it appears as if the duty-officer had inadvertently dropped a slice of sausage on the floor and is now kneeling behind the table and carefully trying to unstick it from the grey floorboard.

When you approach, however, you will see that the hat is empty, that there is no one in the room and no one waiting to greet you at the entrance and relieve you of your outdoor clothes. Or at least your belt and shoelaces.

For a moment you will stand undecided, but a small door inside the duty-room promptly comes to your rescue, hidden from sight by a metal cupboard. That door opens and a man emerges from behind the cupboard; he will eye you and come closer. You will think that he is no different from the others, that he has an unidentified, indecisive face devoid of capacity, just like the others. But it will be only a fleeting impression, for with a swift and seemingly shameful movement the man will reach for his hat. And when he puts it on, concealing the halo impressed on his hair, you will be looking at a totally different face. There will no longer be an unidentified man standing before you; from then on you will be standing before an official on duty.

In silence you will shove the invitation through the heart-shaped aperture in the pane; the duty-officer will glance at it, and then without looking anywhere in particular will speak for the first time as he hands you back your card.

— Floor two, room two hundred and one.

Then he will stretch his hand out towards the bell-push; you will hear the buzzer, and the door, trapped in its steel grating, will stand narrowly open before you.

You will set off upstairs, possessed by a strange sense of calm, which the gate now applauds as it slams metallically behind you. The stairs will creak beneath your tread; you will reflect that the timber has dried out; once, not that long ago, it was wet after a messy job, but now it has dried out; people will pass you by, young men clad in jeans and fashionable shirts, young men no different from their contemporaries out there; the only difference is the problems they have been given to solve, have accepted to solve; one of them turns round after you, Mietek, drop in on me after work; you will look at him in surprise, pardon me, he says, and he runs off on his way. You will be passed by a couple of men in uniform and neither will give you closer scrutiny, not one of them will so much as look back at you, even though the thoughts and hearts and deeds of these people keep you company day and night.

You will climb the stairs. On the second floor you will turn to the left, and the first door you will see will bear the number two hundred and one.

You will check again to see if the number written on your invitation agrees with the number on the door, and you will knock. It opens with lightning speed, as though someone forewarned by telephone by the duty-officer had long been waiting for you there.

You hand him the invitation.

— Identity card, and wait in the corridor — says the man who opened the door.

He will take your identity card, and you will experience another moment of solitude in the dark throat of that building.

Then the door will open and you will be invited inside. The man who took your identity card will let you in and then step towards the exit as though to surprise you from behind.

Then you will ask him.

— May I have the invitation back?

— What for?

— A souvenir.

— Not likely. We're the ones who keep souvenirs.

That sentence is uttered behind your back; you will turn round; another man in an unbuttoned white shirt will be sitting behind the desk with a smile like a bouquet of artificial flowers.

He will hold out his hand to you. Taken by surprise, you will not have the wits or prove capable of refusing.

In your palm you will feel his warm fingers, not even moist, not even hard, not even.

— Please sit down.

— I'd rather stand.

— Please sit down. We'll have a little chat.

You will sit down on a chair placed this side of the desk. You will lean back, and in the protracted silence you wait for the first words.

— You're causing us a lot of trouble.

— I'm sorry.

The man will give you a searching glance, and again will say nothing for a moment.

You will observe that he often casts his eyes downwards, that he sits at an unnatural distance from the desk, and for an instant you will be intrigued. Until you realize that he has an open drawer, at the bottom of which is most likely a card with notes to help him sum you up.

— There's not a single political prisoner in the country.

— There's more.

— There's not one. That is very little. Why should there be more. That way we have peace and quiet. If need be we can always haul in a troublemaker. And talk it all over — brother, what's the point, better chuck it in and so forth. Well, but you're making a nuisance of yourself.

The man settles more comfortably in his chair, lights a cigarette, you will decline when he first holds a pack out in your direction; I don't smoke, we know you smoke, I'm not saying I *never* smoke; he will toss the match into a large glass ashtray on the desk, and will start peering at you again.

— I have two hours set aside for you. We can have a real heart-to-heart. Not to mince matters, as the expression goes.

— So we can.

— Now I have a couple of minor points...

— Is this to be a conversation or an interrogation?

— I'd like to have the answer to a couple of routine questions...

— In that case I presume you'll take an official statement. Right? Or am I mistaken?

The man will glance at you sadly and shake his head.

— Dear me.

Then he will be silent for a while and raise his weary gaze again.

— I had hoped...truly...Have you brought your toothbrush?

— No. I brushed my teeth this morning.

— Teeth should also be cleaned in the evening. And in the morning...

— I know. But I may answer only for the record.

The man will extinguish his cigarette and will strike his side of the desk flatly with his palm. Instantly a side door will open, and another man with the expectancy of a pointer will walk in.

— Sit down at the typewriter. You will take down the official report.

The keys begin to clatter greedily, and you will be able to sit for a moment in silence. Until the man dictates the magic words of the opening. And then you will be amazed to hear your old acquaintance ask your surname, Christian name and various other particulars he has known for a long time. And you will answer him spontaneously.

— What were your activities each day of last week? Starting with Thursday? Do you know what day of the month it was?

You will nod your head without a word; the predatory hands of the man at the typewriter hang in the air, like the hands of a pianist.

— Well?

— I refuse to reply — you hear your own voice.

The face of the man behind the desk drapes itself in sadness. It will also betray the first conditioned reflex of renunciation.

For a moment he will sit with a downcast head, then without a word he will pick up the receiver delicately, like a lily, and dial a number.

— Hello, hello. It's me. Is cell number eight available? Yes? Splendid. *Ciao*.

Then he will look at you reproachfully.

— Why do you cause us so much trouble? You know how much work we have on our plates?

You will remain silent. You will lower your head and at length, with your eyes pinned on the floor, you will say lowly and sadly.

— I know. And I should like to make a statement. With reference to the first question.

— A statement?

— Yes.

The man's face livens up and from somewhere under his collar a smile crawls out.

— Well, I'm all ears. If that's the case.

You will reflect for a moment, and then you will turn towards the man huddled behind the typewriter.

— I hereby testify that I am in no way involved...

In no way involved, murmurs the man at the typewriter, and the greedy keys applaud you.

— ...in no way involved in the explosion that took place four days ago at the foot of Lenin's statue in Nowa Huta.

You will feel the silence descend; the man at the desk will lean his head on his palm and stare aimlessly ahead.

— To hell with it... — he will say, then fall silent.

You will sit quietly for a time, then you will ask apprehensively.

— Am I free now?

— Free? — the man will raise his head. — What? Free?

— May I go home now?

— You may go home.

He will slam the drawer shut in the desk and will sit up closer to the desk-top.

Without a word you will rise and hear another sentence that no longer ends in a question mark.

— And you won't sign an undertaking to keep our conversation secret...

— Frankly...I'd rather not.

He holds out his hand, but only to hand back your identity card. Then he will stick an unlit cigarette in his mouth and nod his head.

You will turn back again in the doorway.

— Well, good-bye then.

— Till we meet again — you will hear him say.

You will close the door behind you. The image of the room will be blurred in the semi-darkness. You will feel yourself separated from those men by solid timber, and that shred of certainty and calm will flicker within you.

And then you will go down the creaking stairs towards the grille of the duty-room, towards the duty-officer, towards the rolling daylight, towards...

Freeze-frame Five

…When did it happen? Could it have been in this country? When?

One can hear the tram coming on the bridge over the Vistula with a groan, looming larger in the vibrating air, suddenly slowing down; blocking its way a barbed line of soldiers, helmets shining with a sickly glow, weapons, boots which prophesy no good; the tram still moves, behind the window the driver, uneven rails shaking him like an epileptic; the tram becomes silent in stopping…

When did it happen? People being pushed out, shouting, forcing those who resist towards the greedy Black Maria. People learning in the wink of an eye to accept the role of convict; silenced heads on their shoulders, back bent, when did it happen?

Narrow interior of the shark-like Black Maria: the student, on whom practised hands have found a pack of cards and a flute — you were going to whistle at the bosses on that pipe, you fucking son-of-a-bitch; I wasn't going to whistle; the heavy air sniggers under the truncheons, diamonds of dust sparkle; the youngster curls up in the corner, his shoulders move in the rhythm of a tango, and the others rest, look through the confiscated cards, shuffle, cut and deal; having a moment to take a breath, one of them turns to the boy; get over here, we need one more player; so move, over here; we're playing battle; move your ass, you son-of-a-bitch…

When did it happen? Was it in this country? The well-fed Black Maria takes its load towards an unknown destination; the tear gas bites into the deserted street…

It has happened here, and now…

Topical Subject

They walked down a street so lifeless it seemed like the aftermath of an evacuation; they walked alone, or not quite alone — a stranger's footsteps loitered behind them; they were walking for his benefit too.

— Well then?

— Well, so I've stopped writing, they were saying, they also said, I was paralyzed by it all. I've no sense of distance. Chaos. Disorientation. Everything that has been so far is over and done with. Blotted out. Vanished. As they were saying. A return to those subjects implies a return to an altered self. They were explaining, I, new, now, I no longer know my own self. A state of exceptional unawareness. I've stopped writing. That unawareness is my private sin. To start writing now, they said, would be immoral. The ancients had an explanation for it. They were saying. Immoral then. Unless I attempted to write about what is going on. In this country in this time I haven't the courage to write. They wondered. I don't know if I'll ever be able to write about it. It was impossible after October. And after December. And after March. Those months are all screwed up in my mind…March was earlier… Couldn't write after June. The change in people then was not even remotely comparable to what has happened now. So it's even more difficult. There are lots of new people. New people have suddenly appeared. They were saying. People have now chosen a new nation. I'll never manage to write about that.

They walked down a street so lifeless it seemed like the aftermath of an evacuation; they walked alone, or not quite alone — a stranger's footsteps loitered behind them; they were walking for his benefit too.

One of them looked round; it was as though he had put his tired head in the warm hollow of his arm, sort of; the stranger lowered his eyes and scrutinized the paving-stones. They were cracked like earth made lifeless by drought.

It was drizzling.

In his hand the stranger held a newspaper folded in half. On one side the word freedom shone brightly in large and anxious characters, and when he seized the flapping wings of his nylon raincoat it looked as though he wanted to shield that word from the predatory locust of the wind.

— See what the newspapers write about now. Just turn round.

— Don't feel like it. I know what they write about. That's not what really matters. They wrote like that before. I used to read the stuff.

A private car emerged slowly from a side street. A doll draped in white with a huge static face was fixed to the front. A quivering eyelid kept drooping over its eye, which glittered as in a fever. The other eye was missing, presumably knocked out in some collision.

— Looks like the television news.

Garlands of yellowish, drenched tissue-paper fluttered in the rear, waving gently; the car floated in their midst like a medusa.

A woman sat inside wreathed in the same smile as the doll on the front; a man in a suit sat bolt upright and black by her side. He had an unseeing stare fixed straight ahead of him, and the corners of his mouth were turned downwards like someone whose face is paralyzed.

— How much longer are we going to write about all this? He was saying. Are no other stories ever going to materialize? That sad creep? And the laughing woman?

— His turn will come. Though as Spinoza said, usually he who laughs last has no front teeth. I don't know if that's always the case. If we don't manage to break through all that, we'll be making a revolution in prose till kingdom come.

The car stopped at the yellow light, and the pale fluttering garlands fell off into the mud like used bandages.

They turned up their collars.

— What smog.

— Bad as Krakow.

— Or Poznan.

— And that smell.

— Time for tea?

— Let's go in.

So in they went; it was cool and dark inside, and a woman was dozing behind the bar. A yellowed fringe of lace was pinned to her forehead, which bulged in a Renaissance manner. Her arm kept twitching.

— Everywhere's free. No place to sit and talk.

— How about here?

The metal stool grated against the floor tiles. The woman at the buffet raised a grudging eyelid.

— Well — she said into space. — Well. But no monkey business.

— May we?

The woman made no reply. For a moment she sat motionless on her high stool, as though she were reciting a brief prayer, then she made her descent. She was so short that she disappeared behind the bar, and the scrap of lace in her hair moving above the terrazzo counter was the only evidence of her progress.

When she came up to the table one of them ordered.

— Two teas.

She turned away.

— Does it come in bags?

— Course it does. What else do you expect?

— With lemon?

— Whatever will you think of next? — she asked with a tortured air.

The door opened and in walked the man who had been following them through the streets that day.

With his newspaper he shook the tear-like drops from his nylon raincoat and fixed his stare upon the pane, beyond which the wall swelled silent with dampness.

— Shall we move? Over there by the bar?

— Right you are.

They stood up, took a few steps and sat down again.

— Let's have a fag.

— Just the thing. One always talks best out of doors.

— Got any matches?

— Somewhere.

The flame hissed in the lighter.

They raised their heads; the man in the nylon raincoat was standing at their side.

— May I give you a light? What...

They looked at him for a moment.

— I smoke too much, actually.

— I can feel something on my lungs.

They put their cigarettes aside, the clear flame subsided in the lighter. With a glassy grey gritting sound the man sat down at the table next to them.

In a clattering of glasses the woman emerged from behind the yellowish curtain that screened off the back quarters of the café. She glanced at them and stopped.

— I'll not serve that table. It's not my pad.

— Then let's move over there.

They got up and with their unlit cigarettes went after the waitress.

— Eight zlotys — she said, setting the glasses on the table.

— What, now?

— When then? So I come chasing after you later? Is that what you think?

She counted the coins and threw them into a faded pouch on her belly. When she passed by the man in the nylon raincoat, he sprang up and stood before her.

— Where's the WC here?

The woman looked up at him for the first time and promptly replied, there isn't one, low grade café — no toilet, what'll you order?

— One coffee.

— There's only lousy ersatz...

— That's OK. One small coffee.

They watched as the man crossed the room again in their direction and sat at his previous table.

— Do you take sugar?

— There isn't any.

— That's all right 'cos I don't either.

They drank a gulpful each.

The man unfolded his newspaper which hid him from sight, and next to the word freedom one of them saw another word; together they made out the name of the newspaper *Soldier of Freedom*.

— It's rotten tea.

— It hasn't brewed. Water's too cold.

— Then we might as well go.

They lit their cigarettes and stood up. They passed the waitress on their way, she was carrying a glass half-filled with yellowish coffee. They glanced once more at the café tables, the bar with its sepulchral terrazzo counter, then went out into the street.

— Let's wait a minute, OK?

— And finish our fags.

They stood in silence, circled by humid swollen smoke. Overhead, grey pigeons careered about in the air. They watched.

Then one of them threw his cigarette-end onto the roadway; one of the pigeons fluttered down and tried to grip the smouldering butt in its beak, but failed to fly away before a speeding car — the damp air gave its wings no support.

They heard the mudguard strike the bird in flight, there was a whirl of feathers; the car was gone.

The pigeon lay in the street; its wings, helplessly outspread, took up really very little space.

— Look. The other one's fucking it.

They saw another pigeon, its feathers bristling, cling-ing to the spine of the dead bird.

Another car sped past. The displaced air jerked the bewildered male, but it did not relinquish its prey.

— Eerie.

They exchanged looks.

— Eerie. What now? Shall it be mine, for me to write about?

— Why yours? We both saw it together.

— Shall we toss for it?

— Or we'll both write. We'll write it together. It's an OK topic. Pity to miss it.

From behind their backs they heard the sound of softly closing doors. The man in the nylon raincoat appeared. In his hand he held the folded newspaper. From one side the word soldier loomed black in large and anxious characters.

— Well? We can go now — one of them said.

— So we can — replied the other.

...along the lifeless street...

Freeze-frame Six

...The woman struggles with the phone booth door, shouting into the receiver, I can't travel to see Mother tomorrow, I am busy for the next two days, and I've got to see the doctor as well...

She stops suddenly, bewildered, as a stranger's voice interrupts firmly — I remind you that you must speak clearly, using simple sentences only.

The woman rushes out, stops, moves again, and then the dark entrance of the church draws her in. She slumps onto a bench, drowned in the waxy silence, and only then, quickly, superstitiously, crosses herself; she sits for a long time, waiting.

People pray silently in the side aisle by the Easter Tomb; a helpless body of Christ on a prison bed, and by him, on a bundle of straw, white paper hearts like snow; children have written the best of their Easter good deeds: I gave up my seat in the tram, I got a good mark at school, I helped a blind man cross the road, I washed the dishes for my mom, I am not using naughty words any more, I gave up my seat on the bus, I've given up lying for good, I stood in line at the butcher's instead of my mother, I promise to work harder at school, I'll look after my little brother, I helped an old lady fetch coal from the cellar, I gave up my seat to a sick man, I shared my orange with a schoolmate...

Shabby Lodgings

To reach the radio you must first decide that you wish to do so, then take your time mustering the strength, then finally force your reluctant hand to the task.

You slowly advance your palm from the warm space that has collected by your side, cautiously expose your fingers beyond the confines of the bedcover, and instantly feel teeming mites of cold assail you.

Your palm wanders ever further from you, then ceases to be yours; of its own accord it moves towards the receiver, rests briefly on the protruding knobs.

Finally your index finger performs the essential act; your hand returns with relief to its former position, back to sleep in the nest.

The radio picks up the second program only. In the beginning there is a long silence, so penetrating that you become convinced the radio will not speak to you this time.

Then a magic eye begins to glow greenly through its receding hood.

Voices begin laboriously to force their way through the coarse, dust-choked material covering the speaker. They are distant, but can be heard with increasing distinctness. It is a music program for children and the producer first gives the theme by tapping out a melody on a piano. Then all repeat the first stanza mechanically and discordantly like so many broken tin toys. The low and resolute tone of the compère makes itself heard above the voices.

The damp air slides down from the windowsill; you try to cover yourself with the skimpy child's coverlet which you found in this rented bed, and you hear the words of the song emerging with difficulty from the speaker.

The sunlight shines through all the sky,
Through all our land so fair,
Our land demands your loyalty,
You are her own true heir.

The frail voices of the children repeat the words with diffidence, gusts of wind flare the curtain, even though the window has not been opened since autumn. Scraps of cotton wool stuffed into the cracks have long since gone grey and now look like sputum.

The sunlight shines through all the sky, through all our land so fair, comes the male solo. A noise is heard outside the high door, pimpled with paint, then footsteps. They stop in the corridor; you hear someone listening; then the hook of the door handle jerks and the door opens to a singsong of hinges; that forty-year-old woman appears in the yellowish rectangle of the door frame.

— Well, yes — she says and breaks off, or else her thought deserts her; she walks over to the stove, opens the door and begins to rattle the poker against the protruding ribs of the grate.

She has her back turned, and when she stoops to peer into the cold cavity, you see the puckered hollow between her thigh and her calf that is like the clenched and toothless mouth of an old woman. Exposed by her hitched-up dressing gown.

— Perhaps I should call the doctor from the welfare center...or what...

You make no reply so as not to squander those chilled words that would explain nothing, but twice over you succeed in executing a motion of the head; it is meant to signify negation, and the woman interprets your motion correctly; so she just shrugs her shoulders helplessly. — At work they don't accept that sort of illness without a doctor's certificate, you must have your L4 form. — I won't go back to that job — you are suddenly amazed to hear your voice; she looks up at you.

— Everyone has to work.

— That's exactly what I'm saying — you hear the reply.

She leaves the room without closing the door behind her; you can see the pregnant darkness of the corridor into which the tinny words of the song now roll, gracelessly, but sounding with greater impact:

The sunlight shines through all the sky,
Through all our land so fair,
Our land demands your loyalty,
You are her own true heir.

The song is lost in the fetid darkness; again you hear footsteps, and the darkness suddenly lights up and glows as though a blazing hoop was rolling over the parquet.

The woman appears carrying a monstrance in her outstretched hand — glimmers of coal scooped a moment ago out of her stove wink and twitch on a tin spade.

She enters the room; the rattling coals vanish inside the stove and stop chattering. Stifled by the cold air, they subside.

She puts the shovel aside, slams the door and fastens it tight. Then, turning away, with one hand she gathers up the dressing gown over her loose breasts and strokes the icy tiles voluptuously with the other.

— Soon it will be nice and warm.

— Very good — you hear a man's voice. — And now I should like to hear the first two lines of the second stanza.

For every day our land's more lovely
Red and white roses everywhere…

The thin voice of a child rings soullessly.

— How about tea — the woman says.

You look at the stove tiles, which are dull as formica, yes, if you could, not a bad idea, you reply.

Her hair is tied behind with a cool violet ribbon.

You half close your eyes to avoid looking at the wedding portrait which hangs above the pallet; a black and white picture with only the mouths of the couple outlined in vampire red; withered smiles cringe between the gleaming teeth.

The keyboard in the speaker bangs out the tune, then the bedraggled chorus breaks out.

For every day our land's more lovely
Red and white roses everywhere…

You raise your eyelids; the woman sets a bleary glass on the chair, puts a newspaper on the bedcover and sits down next to it.

— It's today's — she says.

— I'll wait till it cools. To wash down the powder. It won't go down otherwise.

— Sleeping powders are dangerous.

— They don't even help me to sleep.

She bends over and brutally switches off the radio.

Her eyes roam along the dusty corners of the room in search of some stray thought. Then she draws a spray of air into her lungs; her breasts wander upwards, downwards, shaping the first letter of the alphabet in a shadow on the wall.

You know she is about to speak.

— And yesterday I lined up for seven hours for herring at the deli corner, and some old geezer couldn't take it and snuffed it and the ambulance came but he was dead as a nail. Well, so they wouldn't take him away as they haven't got a coldstore, so they said to call for a van. Somebody covered his face over with *The People's Tribune* and he lay there just like the First Secretary. I won't be able to eat those herrings now.

You grasp the newspaper and set up a barricade of lacey newsprint.

— May I see?

— Frankly it's better out loud — she says. — For what it's worth I can always read it myself. Except that the first and second page were on television yesterday. About antisocialist elements.

— Then what about the centre page? — you ask with some effort.

— Ah. There's an interview with Ryszard Gontarz. Who on earth is Ryszard Gontarz…aha, here we are,…publicist and playwright.

— You see.

— …And playwright. Some time ago I saw a splendid show at the Warsaw Citadel commemorating the anniversary of Felix Dzierzynski's birth. You are the author of the scenario. How is it that when your writing to date has dealt only with contemporary problems you should now turn to a historical subject? The question was put by Anna Klodzinska. Now for the answer. In the public view Felix Dzierzynski is a figure cast in steel, who never wavered or yielded to any human frailty. I wanted to depict him not just on the grand scale but as an extremely sensitive man, impressionable and romantic. Hence the title, *Romantic Revolutionary*.

She hides herself from your eyes with the newspaper screen. Outside the window the light is already dispersing, the day is on the ebb. You cannot see her, but you can feel her leaning, resting on her elbow; her breast slouches against your foot and lends it some warmth.

— Let's try something else — the woman whispers. — How about a poem? Here's a poem. Poets' corner. Bohdan Chorazuk — the words rattle softly like chick-peas.

We have a mine of gold at hand
The ideal aggregate
Of Politburo members
And honest workers' sweat

— ...no, it won't do... — she says shamefacedly.

She puts aside the cool pages, she is silent; the heat of her fingers radiates up your knee.

— Here's a travel article. Stand beneath the Eiffel Tower on Panorama Street. Coloured photographs against a background of the Eiffel Tower, the Arc de Triomphe or the Egyptian pyramids without leaving the homeland may be ordered at the new shop shortly to open by the Polifoto Cooperative in Panorama Street. Lifelike scenery and proper posing will give your photos that authentic look. To allow for full preparation of background and model, the entire process will last about half an hour...

She stops reading, remaining screened; you stretch

out your hand. For a moment it wanders among pockets of air and then chances on a shape. You press and again you hear the muffled voices.

And through our homeland far and wide
The youthful fires are burning there.

Her hand proceeds higher and even higher; you hear the rustle of her motion; the woman leans her head on your knees and you feel the desperate pulsing of the artery in the hollow of her neck; she says something in a hasty lustreless voice that fades away.

You are at a distance, watching, your eyes rake your body in unastonished scrutiny.

Footsteps can be heard outside the window; the woman straightens up without withdrawing her hand. — It's my old man back from work, she says, I recognize his step.

She rises slowly and pushes your glass towards you with a gesture full of weariness. You see the cool violet ribbon that binds her hair.

The door closes with a soft heave, and then as through a fog you hear the two metallic clinks of a lock being opened.

You raise yourself on your elbow and peel the cellophane shell from the sleeping powder. You place it in your mouth and wash it down with watery tea.

From the corridor voices are heard balancing as on a tightrope, then everything falls silent and the flurried woman slips through the chink between darkness and light, two gentlemen have come from the Committee and say they want to know why you've been away from work for the last four days and whether you're ill and they want to see you, they're waiting out there.

You sit up on the bed, the coverlet falls away from

your chest, but breathing's none the easier for that.

— Well then…that means…they can't come…I refuse to see them. Kindly tell them that I haven't been to work for four days because I've spent the last four days eating my little red book page by page each contribution stamp every seal my surname photograph and that the worst of the lot was the cover, because it was so hard but I chewed it very thoroughly and now it will take me to the end of my life to digest it and I'll never fully digest it…neither the covers nor the colour nor my own name which I've swallowed. So I have all that to digest and I shall no longer have time to go to work. Well, and tell them to get along without me and go back where they came from. There's no question of their coming in here…'Raus…

— Am I to repeat your exact words? — she asks in alarm.

— My exact words.

She turns slowly away and you hear her whispering, she repeats the words so as not to get them wrong, he hasn't been to work because he's spent the last four days eating his little red book page by page every contribution stamp every official seal his surname photograph, well but the worst of the lot was the cover, because it was so hard, but he chewed very thoroughly and now it will take him until the end of his life to digest it though he'll never fully digest the covers or the…, she screens you from the darkness with the leaf of the door. You turn up the radio which receives only the second program and you wrap yourself in the child's coverlet.

— And now the whole stanza. Nicely now.

Beads of dust flicker round the box, a voice spills from the speaker.

For every day our land's more lovely,
Red and white roses everywhere,
And through our homeland far and wide
The youthful fires are burning there.

You feel you are falling, you feel how the sputter of sleep muddies your thoughts for the first time after your own hundred days, you are falling, becoming brittle, the thud of your dry heart turns cold, you are falling...

Freeze-frame Seven

…Planes that take off from this airport for the metropolis of the East sometimes land on the other side of the world, in West Berlin.

These few subdued people will soon board a plane, which they will hijack to Frankfurt; they will stay nearby, waiting for an onward flight, and until the moment of their irrevocable landing on American soil, none of them will call himself an *emigré*.

More than one empty bottle of Russian vodka will fly out the window of an expensive boarding house as they wait.

— A pal of mine phoned yesterday, asking me not to forget to bring a bag of 20-zloty coins because they fit the vending machines over there in place of 5 or 2-mark pieces; he said they've already run out of Polish money. He must be crazy, but I heard his voice quite clearly.

The check-in will soon be finished and the tired air hostess can hardly look at the passenger talking to her; later she will recognize his face from Kodacolor prints.

These people, soon to be hijacked, pretend to be calm; in their sweaty fingers they clutch these strange, brand-new passports…

Journey

The elevator door closed suddenly like a mouth in mid-speech; he was alone inside with that shred of a woman teetering on a dilapidated crimson stool. She seemed asleep, leaning her head against the cool wall of the cabin; he was silent, pervaded by a sense of calm.

The woman dozed, eyes fixing on him through a blurred gaze. Her half-open lids quivered like acacia petals.

That sense of calm did not elicit any surprise in him; he had expected it and had been waiting for its gentle wave ever since the moment he had first thought of the palace. Once when he came out of the station, he had raised his eyes and seen that pile looming out of the fog of early dawn; it looked as though a mischievous Stalin had shat in the middle of the gigantic square; he had then recalled that a ride to the top cost only a few zlotys.

Now he was standing in this small cage and felt pervaded by a sense of calm.

The hand of the sleepy woman rose grudgingly towards the lever, his feet began to feel the pressure of the floor; he raised his head and saw figures lighting up one after the other, one floor after the other, in the grey squares above the door.

He held his hand in his pocket and with his fingers

touched the oval disc the cloakroom attendant had given him down below when he handed in his jacket; I don't need a check, he said to the one-armed man as he placed his jacket on the marble slab, what do you mean, really, the one-armed man looked at him; how can I give you back your coat, I mean really; he vanished for a moment behind a screen of lifeless transpiring garments, then threw him the token; it rolled along the slippery stone and fell rattling to the floor. He did not want to prolong the conversation. He was waiting patiently for the peace that would shortly descend. He swiftly bent down to pick it up and stuffed it in his pocket. Now he felt it with his fingers.

— How long've you been working this thing? — he said to the woman who quivered at her post like a black spider in a bath of boiling water.

— How long you say? — she said to herself, unable to understand the question. — How long. Time out of mind. All me life. Time out of mind.

— And you don't get bored.

— Bored you say. Work's varied. First 'un goes up. Then 'un goes down. Sometimes 'un goes to the thirty-second. Other times 'un goes to the eleventh. Varies...

His feet felt the uniform pressure of the elevator floor. He remained silent, kept peering at the chequerboard of floor numbers. With each successive flash he climbed higher, further, closer.

— And anyway four years ago on Women's Day they gave a bonus, not to be claimed back, two hundred zloties. But there's no justice. That bitch on the second shift got two hundred and thirty. There's no justice — the woman suddenly uttered into the void. Then she raised to him her eyes, rabbit-like from lack of sleep and lined with little red veins, and for a moment he saw despair and hatred in those eyes; then they were again hooded by the lids.

Thoughts had ceased to pain him. His fingers now sought out the oblong card in the recess of his pocket; it was the return ticket he had had to buy down at ground level.

— A ticket up to the terrace. One way please.

— One way only — how on earth — the ticket-man looked at him, and his arm kept making convulsive movements as though he were trying to block his ear. Are you going to return from the sights up there by the stairs? That big world?

— Yes. One way only please.

— There ain't no one-way tickets. There's only return tickets. You can get one-way tickets on the tram if you fancy. But not for our sightseeing here. But you can on the tram — he said rumbling with spasmodic laughter. He took a long time to calm down as he stroked his cheek with his arm.

His fingers now began to crumple the ticket, crush it, shred it. They moved of their own accord, without his being aware.

The walls of the elevator were scribbled over with dates, initials, place names, I was here, in this elevator I lost my cherry to Lis, We the Union of Polish Youth are unafraid, Gomulka is a big little prick — school teacher from Nysa, Krakow men are pricks not Poles, Babiuch has bedroom eyes, You can keep your student mag — give us back *Plain Speech*, better Kania than Vanya, I love Marycha Robaszkiewicz, the queen of Kozalin, Scoutmaster's gone — fucking's on, Danka — quit fooling before they start screwing,

Grabbed meat, filched bread, guess his name — it's our Ed, Confederation of Independent Poland are runts. Some words were written in ball point, others scratched with sharp implements.

— When do they do it? — he asked, running his nail along the crooked contour of an engraved heart.

— Can't stop 'em. When you're catnapping straightaway they pull out some nail and they're at it again. The worst is when they're against the system because then they pick on me. Yes, as if it was my fault the system's the way it is. Can't stop 'em. There's no one doesn't want to leave his mark as a memento-like.

— I don't.

— You do-o-o-nt? — she broke out into a voiceless laugh. 'Cos I'm watching your hands. Everyone does. But when they comes and picks on me I put the blame on that bitch from the second shift. Four years ago on Women's Day they gave two hundred zlotys unreclaimable bonus. But there's no justice. The bitch on the second shift got two hundred and thirty...

His feet felt the pressure from the elevator floor imperceptibly diminish. Already he was high and close. The shaggy palm of the woman wandered towards the lever.

He raised his eyes. His last box with the floor number lit up sympathetically, and that was it.

— There then — said the woman.

— Have you ever been on the terrace?

For a moment her astonished lids revealed two eyes streaked like marble balls.

— Why the blummin' hell should I. There's a howling gale up there, somethin' awful. What, to get me head blown off?

— Don't ask me. To see the view...

— I'm all right where I is. In the warm. But there's no justice.

The door wheezed open.

The dim lightbulb gave way to the day.

He felt an increasing sense of relief, a volatile lightness, but he turned his head back again to look at the necrotic woman.

She remained silent and motionless.

He withdrew his gaze and went on his way.

He passed the bend in the lofty corridor. And then the daylight hit him.

Space unexpectedly made itself felt.

He was not looking; he could not see the greedy clouds of fog crowding in, he could not hear the muffled echoes from below.

He moved forward then stopped. His eyelids were lowered. He was expecting nothing.

The terrace was empty, tousled by gusts of rain.

He took a few light steps and forgot about everything once and for all. Only his feet sensed the diligent unbroken pulse of the ground.

He felt the impact of stone — the humid barrier held him up for another brief moment.

Then he opened his eyes again.

The terrace was immense. It was not situated on the highest storey, and the roof above it was supported by heavy concrete pillars.

After he had looked more carefully he realized that a shiny impassable steel netting was spread out tightly between the columns, the barrier and the roof. He noticed the clear translucent gleams of liquid fog on the metal.

He stood rooted to the spot and stared at the steel netting.

A low cloud rode up, clasped him in a clammy white stillness but could not lift him into space. The steel netting made that impossible. He stood immersed in the cloud and painfully recollected everything....

Freeze-frame Eight

...The psychiatrist is pouring vodka down his throat without blinking an eye and is talking, his hair greying to the right, asymmetrically.

— I am giving in my notice, I am changing my profession.

The glass in front of him is full again, a crystal-like drop bursting on its rim. — As a doctor I cannot help anybody anymore, that makes me grey on the right side, asymmetrically; a patient tells me, I am under surveillance, nowhere can I be alone, they are everywhere; they put a bug in my home and as if that was not enough, they listen in to my telephone conversations, so I stopped making calls, they even open my letters, even postcards they read, everything, and when I go out into the street, they want to poison me with gas; simply, they want to gas me; they are everywhere; and the right side of my hair is getting greyer from it and I wish to reply to him, that I also have the same symptoms, exactly the same, that it is only a harmless persecution mania, which will pass, that it is easy to cure and he should not bother about it too much; both of us would be cured of this mania; yesterday I was on duty in the emergency ward and I was taken to an unsuccessful suicide case, it was an activist, he had been in hiding for months and his nerves could take no more; he cut minor veins, but I knew that tomorrow, or the day after tomorrow, he would do it for real; inescapable, and from the ambulance, by the radiophone, I contacted the police and I reported it, because prison, that is his only rescue and therapy; they said they are on their way to get him and thanked me, and at that moment I understood that this was my last day working in this profession. — He is pouring vodka down his throat without blinking an eye, placing the chilled glass against his hair…

No Sound of Footsteps in the Treetops

A deserted square with a naked tree in its midst, standing dead still because sham gusts of wind can take no grip on its scant branches.

The sky above the square is ashen and congealed in space as though an extinct part of our planet were mirrored in it.

A row of posts kept in spotlight from dusk to sluggish dawn; a row of posts in a hoar-frost of light, each decked in a crown of thorns, a steel girdle with sharp spikes pointing downwards, secured at the height of upraised arms; if any prisoner in a fit of madness wanted to climb above the flat roofs, those spikes would come to meet him.

Rows of barracks; iron bars gleam inanely in the windows; barracks are everywhere, at all the corners of this moderately-sized universe. They are separated from the square by a high netting crowned with barbed wire.

The square is deserted; not long ago people wandered along the small loop of pathway; a mist of exhalation and stillness rose gradually above them, boots kicked up a dust of snow. Timorous minutes of the allotted stroll slipped past.

There were twenty of them, perhaps thirty. Several cells.

The guards who followed them with hate-filled eyes cowered in the sharp air; one of them hid behind the metal netting; it gave him a spot of shelter without obscuring the view.

The men wandered in file and in silence. Boots kicked up a dust of snow, brief minutes for walking slipped swiftly away.

They had turned up here for war to be waged in peace.

For war to break out on a grim December day, enemies had to be identified. For doing battle, the last battle for so many years, an enemy army had to be found.

Those and those too were called the enemy. They were made prisoners before being told that war had broken out. Prisoners were taken first in this war, and war was declared afterwards. Before the tanks began to roll through the squares, the prisoners were already behind walls, surveyed by towers bristling with guards.

Before the battle the prisoners were taken.

Those who until recently had been roving loose on a tightly watched rein were invented, so the war could go on.

The dead and the missing were also designated for that war. The dead and the missing were not invented. Their crosses are real, as real as the crosses of the brave.

A deserted square and a naked tree. Another few frail minutes will fall away, and the guards will escort the next group out. Then they will cower in the sharp air, and one of them will hide behind the metal netting which will give him a spot of shelter without obscuring the view.

The prisoners will wander in silence. A woman will suddenly wake up in a faraway house. A guard will peer around suspiciously.

The war goes on; beyond the wall the forest returns to life in the ascending light, but there is no sound of footsteps in the treetops.

Freeze-frame Nine

…Patches of steel-coloured paint on the cold walls of the houses cover the slogans of an earlier time.

People sneak out at night with buckets of bright paint to liquidate those grey patches of bad conscience, a constant reminder of the slogans underneath.

With quick brush strokes they paint some crooked houses, hang yellow suns above them, and fill the freshly drawn path with shapeless, small-headed human figures.

So by the time the morning painfully awakes, everything looks as if unseen gangs of unruly children have decorated the walls of their beloved town.

A man is spat out of the bus, his empty gaze arrested for a moment by the picture of a cheerful gnome; he shakes himself, wipes his forehead, and with this careless movement knocks off his beret, which is too big for his head. Taking it up from the dust, he seems to genuflect to a passer-by; whom he suddenly grabs by the sleeve, and into whose eyes he gazes beseechingly.

— Please, Sir. Which way to the United States, Sir?

— Oh…er…first to the right, then straight on. Let go of my sleeve. Yes, it's somewhere there, turn left and then straight on.

— Which way? I'm not with you.

— Oh, come off it…

White Night

It is a frosty day; an acrid frost crushes the thorny spikes in the air.

It is a bleak, hard, Muscovite December day.

The day is self-evident, but the man stops suddenly amid the snowflakes and simply cannot believe; how is it possible, he repeats, how is it possible; the edge of his upraised collar freezes against his cheek, it is impossible, another war; a gust of wind parts the white curtain from behind which the bus stop, like an aquarium, looms into sight; a bunch of lonely people stare at him; how is it possible, another war; what shall I tell the family, what shall I give them to eat, another war, and I haven't got a good *Kennkarte** ...another...

People stare at him; a storm of white flakes swirls impatiently above his head. They shift their weight from one leg to the other in search of warmth; behind their backs the glass wall quivers and rings. On it a harsh sentence has been billposted: the proclamation of martial law. A relentless hand has crossed through those words and substituted the Nazi formula — *Bekanntmachung*.

Kennkarte. The special identity card issued to Poles during the Nazi occupation in World War Two.

72

Other words and phrases are scrawled on the glass wall of the aquarium, as though in a duel; TV lies; Polish People's Republic = Leonid's private ranch; KOR = Jews; we demand the registration of Solidarity without changes in the Statute; we'll avenge Katyn; the Economic Aid Council gives everything to Russia and shit to Poland; KOR = Bonn spies. Another sentiment on the side wall expands with every hour; initially only a few black words, the eagle will not be vanquished by the crow. Then further revisions are made: the crow will croak before the eagle's vanquished, the fucking crow will croak before the eagle's vanquished, the fucking croaking crow will blow before...

One must be cautious, very cautious, the man repeats, one must be cautious, there could be a round-up any minute, any minute...it's no laughing matter...there's a war on...

People stare at him, war, war, someone mutters, we know it's war; sooner or later there had to be war, I mean how long could they be expected to wait, bloomin' red spiders; thirty years ago they issued us an ultimatum, yes or no, head or tails, you can't have it both ways, communism and belt up, or else war — the choice is yours...so then it's war...

But to do it to your own people, your *own* people, for a Pole to declare war against Poles...I mean...a woman whispers through whitened lips; Poles my ass, you'd first have to sew collars onto their Russian peasant shirts to make them look like Poles, the motherfuckers. Real Polish army collars.

— What sort of people are they...what sort of people can they be...yet they say the father of one of the top-brass died in Katyn...incredible...for a son to fall so low.

— Died in Katyn...He didn't die, he killed himself. Got drunk and fell off a watch tower. You'd better listen properly if you're going to listen at all...

— There could be massacres, the solitary man speaks up; there could always be massacres; a gust of wind presses his words into a bend in the wall.

— He's standing out there in the cold — someone from the aquarium says — he'll freeze to death in that frost. Hey mister. Come under the roof, come under the Shelter.

His mouth moves, but the words cannot pass through the numb glass; mister, come under the roof, it's warmer here, someone repeats tapping his finger against the pane; transfixed with sounds the man suddenly doubles up from cold, is screened for a moment by a shutter of wind and snow; an instant later the air clears again, but the man has gone; he has been swallowed up by a protective gateway.

The people in the aquarium tread down the snow with their feet.

— The spring will be ours — someone says. — I saw it written, the soldiers were rubbing the words off a tank, the winter's yours, the spring is ours, some kid painted it on, they were rubbing it off. The spring will be ours...so they say...

The words freeze to the glass, snowflakes twirl in a cradle of wind, a young woman's face comes alive inside her collar.

— You are cold — says someone in a crimson plastic coat that creaks with every word. — They hijacked that bus to Sweden, didn't they? Feeling cold?

— Freezing.

— You'd soon warm up again...if a real man cuddled

you — says the man, and he starts to shake with ribald laughter; the crimson armour creaks in the snow.

— The real men are in prison now — the woman replies, and the crimson plastic goes still.

Then out of the silence a bus suddenly emerges. The red smudge grows bigger, and the motionless crowd returns with difficulty to life, as in the moment after awakening.

— We've waited an hour and forty minutes.

— We're lucky it's here...It might not have come at all...with the war...

The bus proceeds without speed or sound; its wide windscreen is frozen over. The driver presses his white brow against the pane and studies the road ahead.

Then the front doors open like an accordion, but the little crowd of people in the aquarium is again rooted to the ground. A man appears on the step followed by a young boy. They look like father and son. It looks as though the son is leaning on his father, and the father leading his son. The man pulls the boy after him; the boy's hand repeats every movement of the man's hand. A moment later they are standing in a lather of snow. Within the frame of the door the blurred faces look like part of a group portrait. The man stoops again, and with his free hand picks up some white papers from the step of the bus which he hurriedly stuffs into his pocket; one flies out of his fingers and falls breathless at the feet of the waiting crowd.

Leaflets...someone says in a whisper, he was distributing leaflets; the boy plods after the man. Their hands tense up and one can see now that they are joined by handcuffs.

Those waiting watch in silence. Then the young

woman speaks in a stifled voice, speaks with difficulty — do something, do something, do...

The image of the man and the boy is softened by the innocent whiteness; a blister of warm steam swells in the open door of the bus; the people huddle inside without looking back; submissively they do not turn back, but retreat into the comfy interior. The young woman remains alone at the bus stop with her head downcast; the man and the boy have vanished.

The doors close, bursting the bubble of warmth; the bus drifts away.

The woman stands stock-still. A leaflet lies at her feet, but she cannot bend to pick it up; she can no longer move.

Freeze-frame Ten

…This town's Victory Square has lost its last battle; now it is only a fragment of space, closed in by a high hermetic fence; some time ago people were laying flowers here, creating a flower cross in memory of the dead, those killed by a treacherous assassin. Now the only symbol is the dead Hotel Victoria, in front of which the tout quickly tries to get rid of his zloties, buying dollars or other hard currency; he whispers into the emptiness and looks at the solitary tart; a secret policeman attempts to get her — do you think you can screw me because of your badge, you idiot?

A bit further on, under the weathered statue of Victory, whose sword has wasted away, a bus stops, and through the dirty front window one can see the guide. His lips move silently, forcing some words down the microphone; behind the glass, people, motionless like crabs, some of them in sullied sleep, others mindlessly stare ahead…

Day of Mist and Cloud

It is morning, but the wartime day cannot emerge from half-darkness.

The tumid air subsides heavily and the snow alone emits a kind of low gleam. People's faces are plunged in shadow.

The innocent white of the crossroads is scarred by the caterpillar-tracks of tanks. They have rolled past many times in the night, sowing alarm more than usual, boring their way through the city. In two days it will be Christmas.

One of the tanks has come to a dead halt at the crossroads — broken down or abandoned by its crew, no one can tell.

There is a bitter frost. A metal basket full of throbbing coals stands by the wall of a house whose inmates do not come near the windows. Several soldiers stoop over the brazier, stretching their hands toward it like beggars; the green flames pulse between their fingers.

Others helplessly surround a car they have just stopped; the NCO peers greedily inside, then in the back he discovers a fuel can, an object banned for several days now; he pulls it out and opens it, and a yellow stream trickles along the curb; the driver turns his head aside and does not look.

The car drives off, stillness descends, withdrawn passers-by flounder in silence; a mud-coloured police van, known as a disco, lies in ambush by the tank. It has not yet grabbed its fill today.

The militiamen prowl the neighbourhood, leer insolently into faces, check papers, rummage through handbags. Sometimes they lead someone towards the van, and then the eyes of the onlookers come back to life, filled with curiosity and fear.

Two uniformed men stand facing the wall with arms upraised, as though they are about to be shot on the instant, ineffectually trying to paint over an inscription that sprouted during the night. Two words persistently rise to the paint's surface: *Cunta Junta*.

The soldiers gathered at the rhythmic fire suddenly turn round; a woman has come up to them. They peer at her grey coat, at the ashes of hair tumbling onto her shoulders from under a black headscarf; there is confusion in their eyes; she speaks to them slowly, fervently; they avoid her gaze, they are silent; any moment now the NCO will appear with several militiamen; they lead the old woman away, and she offers no resistance.

The soldiers hang their heads lower still, but the brazier throws intense heat and light on their foreheads and they have nowhere to hide; the automatic pistols hanging at their belts knock against their sides, rub painfully, excruciatingly.

The face of a man about to be swallowed up by the voracious police van is white as snow; the Christmas tree he was gingerly carrying has been knocked out of his arm; it is now being looked over, evaluated, assessed with a proprietary eye by a corporal. Then it is raised from the ground, shaken free of white dust and set up in a secluded corner. The corporal will guard it, it will be his.

At the bus stop people are huddled in a crowd; they look grey in the glassy milklike fog, they are waiting...

— It was different during the occupation, it was...The Germans used to kill us, but they let us get on with life...

— I tell you. Before the war there was a great hue and cry, Jews to Madagascar, Jews to Madagascar. We're the ones that ought've buggered off there. I mean it.

There is suddenly some traffic at the crossroads, the air vibrates, a minibus draws up to the curb. A cameraman leaps out, then an officer; they help a woman, opulent sheepskin, a carmine foam of smile on her lips, to extricate herself from the snug interior; someone obligingly offers her his arm, the cameraman selects a spot; with a snicker she flumps down finally in the wool-like snow.

In her fingers she grips several red carnations, which are shrivelled by the frost in an instant, and a gramophone record in a coloured sleeve.

She now poses in the shadow of the motorcar, waiting; words spill quietly from her mouth like beads; we Polish women and Polish mothers...we owe it to *you* that peace has prevailed in the streets of our towns and in our homes..civil war...and the villages...you have prevented...you have...counter-revolution...we shan't renounce the achievements of socialism...

The soldiers assembled over the meagre source of fire also stand still, their outstretched palms stung by the fateful, opaline sparks; two officers stride towards them, the cameraman makes himself comfortable.

The officers spot out the tallest among them, give him a good looking over; how's service, one of them asks, yes Sir, the soldier draws to attention.

— As you know Christmas will soon be with us. You lads have been selected to receive a gift and a modest soldier's, you know, posy of flowers, from the hands of our representative of Polish motherhood; seeing as you perform your duty, you know, in exemplary fashion and carry out the assignments with which you are entrusted, you will have the honour of being immortalized by Polish television and shown to the general public on the silver screen; are you ready, the citizeness representing Polish motherhood is waiting, truth, women's organizations. Stand tall, soldier.

And the soldier takes one step back, he wants to say something, but no one is listening to him, so he stands motionless as in a dream; there is bustle around him, the camera hisses venomously; his colleagues draw warily aside to avoid that eye; the soldier sees before him the smudge of face grinning vapidly, on account of Christmas we Polish women and Polish mothers...we owe it to *you* that peace has prevailed in the streets of our towns and in our homes...civil war...and the villages...you have prevented...you have...counter-revolution...we shan't renounce the achievements of socialism...

The soldier thinks frantically, no answer comes into his head; he can now see the woman's broad back and mechanically repeats behind her, at the colonel's orders we launched a spontaneous collection on behalf of the flood victims...

There is no more camera or microphone; the minibus moves off; through its window the bunch of red carnations scattered on the seat can be seen; the soldier lowers his head and finds that he is holding a record in a coloured sleeve; but they've made an ass of you, someone says from the sidelines; he tosses the record on the seething ants' nest of coal; a mute black smudge spills out…

The tank at the crossroads returns suddenly to life; the engine gasps for breath, and the armour-plating begins to quiver delicately; the tumid air subsides heavily…

Freeze-frame Eleven

...The small deserted square has become a true bazaar and the woman, wrapped in a cocoon of rags, huddles alone — a handful of wilted carrots scattered at the feet of politicians on the front page of a newspaper; are the carrots good enough for children, somebody asks timidly; sweet as honey, comes the emphatic reply, sweet as honey.

— How fresh is the cabbage?

— Fresh as we are.

— Lovely eggs, tiny ones, nice!

— Or else I'll hang myself on that belt maybe — says a man with a coarse laugh, having nothing more to sell.

One vendor has displayed bright cookbooks on his stall, full of forgotten notions and fragrances, and nearby in a shop called The House of Shoes a man, staring avidly into the lifeless face of the salesclerk, shows her his coupon.

— I fell down coming from work. And when I was nearly home, I almost slipped again. Most probably because my shoes are worn out. So I ask you, what am I supposed to walk around in?

— Oh, go away, sir — the salesclerk stirs in her lethargy — do go away...

Bitter Red Star

For two days now they had been sitting face to face; the wind had driven in an early dusk and the bulb glowed shamelessly; they sat face to face, divided only by the yellowish desk.

He sat with his back to the unprotected wall, behind his back the plain-clothes man had a metal cupboard; the light glimmered faintly on its polished door.

They had been sitting face to face for two days now, the plain-clothes man was tired, and another man in another room was now working on the verdict, for which they had both been waiting for the last two hours.

There was an air of calm; the plain-clothes man perused an old newspaper with outdated photographs of leaders who had been degraded in a single night; the last two days had created a certain intimacy between them; they were no longer strangers, and although one of them knew next to nothing about the other, neither would now be able to pass the other indifferently in the street.

They had been cooped up in this room together for two days; the plain-clothes man had ceased to bo a real oppressor, and he had ceased to be a real victim; fot the plain-clothes man he was an inconvenience, a thorn in the flesh, as their mutual contract had often been undermined over the past two days; the plain-clothes man now regretted he had failed to hold up his shield, had lowered it and come out of cover too soon, had lost his distance, let the distance be interrupted; he had lost some of his ascendancy, and lost it forever.

They sat face to face in silence, smoking cigarettes; as he kept fumbling for matches the plain-clothes man held out a lighter in his hand, and now he could not forgive himself for having been tricked into the gesture.

Yesterday had been different; when they took him handcuffed from home and down the elevator, it was totally different; they had absolute power over him. The cage quivered softly; when he slightly shifted his position, the drawing of a gallows leered up from behind his shoulders; the words Polish United Workers' Party were hanging from the noose; they spotted the drawing, exchanged looks; ha ha, one of them said, that's witty, that is, and instinctively he loosened his collar; they exchanged looks but they were too embarrassed to erase it, and that was their first mistake the plain-clothes man now realized.

The cage walls quivered; the elevator stopped at one of the floors, an elderly man opened the door. Keep out, it's the militia, one of them barked, the man stopped dead in his tracks, as at a distant memory slowly raising his hands; the cage resumed its journey.

Then they sat in this room; that was their first day; the plain-clothes man put some questions, colleagues of his kept dashing into his room, how's it going, has he or hasn't he begun to give evidence, is he talking or isn't he, they kept asking, and then they would dash out again. He somehow doesn't want to talk, the plain-clothes man replied, it's rather tricky, he doesn't feel inclined.

— He doesn't feel inclined, eh? Then we'll see to it that he does — and they promptly rushed out, and there was not a shade of privacy between the two of them; with those brief appearances during the first hours they could operate officially and distantly.

— Any progress? Is he talking?

— He refused — the plain-clothes man replied; his moustache had a downwards droop which gave him an expression of immeasurable sadness; as they walked down long corridors to their present room he noticed that one in two of the young men sported the moustache that had been launched at the Gdansk shipyard eighteen months before.

— He's refusing to talk?

— Seems like it.

— Here's a piece of paper and a pen. Give a precise account of the last two weeks. Day by day. A precise account — he struck the sheet of paper against the table top, and then a sprinkling of ash glided down on a thread of light; he observed its descent and, for no reason, they followed his eyes; silence fell for a moment.

— You have a good knowledge of French — the plain-clothes man said.

— No…Pity. I don't. A few hazy notions. A bit of German. *Halt. Hende hoch*…From war films…

— You don't know French? Then how did you establish contact with the *service ronsainement*? What? You know what it is? Do you mean to say you don't…

— What it is?

— You don't know? Let me refresh your memory. It's French espionage.

— There's no French espionage — he replied — That much I know for sure.

— No espionage, what do you mean? How can there be no espionage when there is? — the plain-clothes man slowly uttered, and fell silent.

— Here. On this paper you will give an exact account of your last two weeks. Day by day — the second man tapped his finger against the white paper.

— I refuse.

— So it's no?

— No it is.

The second man turned round and dashed out of the room; silence settled and lasted an instant; the door half opened again.

— You have three minutes. Stopwatch in hand. You have three minutes. Three minutes to make up your mind. Are you for the opposition or aren't you? Make up your mind — he flung his fist forward as though to strike, but wished merely to expose the watch on his wrist.

— You have three minutes.

He fixed his gaze intently on the window; the armoured car in the frozen courtyard down below had broken down and several soldiers were bustling helplessly around it; the lifeless town lay some distance beyond; a pile of snow was hardening on the pavement; a man stopped forlornly in the street, as if he could not find the way in his own town; in a bathroom a pensive woman was slowly washing her hair.

— One minute gone.

He said nothing; you have two minutes to go. Make up your mind. Are you with the opposition or aren't you? again he was silent; a frozen drop twanged on the pane.

— What are you staring at that window for? What?

What is there to stare at? — the other one asked.

— There are sparrows screwing on the windowsill. In winter...

Again the door slammed and they were left alone; you received dollars, we've got receipts in the cupboard, the plain-clothes man said, then fell silent.

— Dollars from French Intelligence?

— You know what I mean. Francs.

Now they were sitting face to face; the second day was beginning to slip away and the plain-clothes man felt that now he must speak.

— I went to Hungary. Last year...

— And?

— Prices have gone up. It's expensive.

Silence again settled between them; the plain-clothes man raised his head and stared at the ceiling; his pistol was rubbing nastily under his armpit.

— Salami, a hundred and ten forints. Ham, a hundred and ten. Cigarettes, fifteen. Mouth-organ, two hundred. Shoes, a few hundred.

— And matches?

— Matches? Don't know.

— You mentioned cigarettes.

— I have a lighter.

— What does wine cost?

— Ten forints.

— Tea?

— Packet or glass?

— Glass.

— Don't know. I took my own tea bags with me.

— What does a shirt cost?

— Two hundred and fifty.

— Did you go to the cinema?

— No.

— Really?

— Real... — he glanced at him in astonishment and fell silent; he was tired, and he longed for their ways to part.

He glanced at the plain-clothes man; not that long ago you were putting opponents of Gierek's regime behind bars.

— Well, yes. Of course.

— Where's the logic? You put them in prison then, you're still putting them in prison now. Then you lock Gierek up. And a couple of his cronies. Ultimately were those who opposed Gierek right or not?

— Well, sort of. Gierek's inside.

— Then how do you figure it all? Which side is guilty?

The plain-clothes man observed his desk at some length.

— You see. You see, we are basically fighting for the same cause...for the same cause...Only we fight from opposing camps. But we are fighting for the same cause...After all...

The door then opened, and the other officer stood on the threshold; he held an innocent white paper in his hand; the plain-clothes man gazed at him with hope and gratitude.

— So? — he exclaimed as he stood up; he stalked several paces from the desk, only then did he feel more at ease — so?

— We're taking him to Bialoleka. It's all signed.

— That's good. Off we go. Is there a car?

— Waiting downstairs.

— So everything's in order?

— Everything's OK.

— Good. Get your coat on — he tossed over his shoulder.

He stood up; he slung his jacket over his numbed shoulders and drew himself up to full height.

— Should we handcuff him? — the plain-clothes man asked; he spoke at a brisk pace now; he'd returned to routine.

— Whatever for? He can't escape. He's got nowhere to go.

— Well? — the plain-clothes man glanced at him. — Well?

He stretched out his hand and struck the switch with the flat of his palm; the bulb ceased to throb and hum; the corridor before him was full of light; he stood erect and slowly stepped into the glowing bright rectangle, into the chasm of a well, into a storm of locusts.

Freeze-frame Twelve

…The pavement in the square in front of the Royal Castle stinks sourly of fresh tear gas, from the narrow side street rumbles a herd of wheelchairs; rickety ones, pushed by soldiers, chairs bounce and rattle; each soldier has at breast level two bewildered eyes, shining like medals.

The expedition, full of pitfalls, reaches its goal: the bus waiting at the curb, behind it a military van; in the eyes of the cripples relief flickers; the soldiers quicken their pace, driving away the pigeons stupified by gas.

They surround the bus, grab the invalids in their arms; cap-peaks covering their shame, they crowd in front of the bus door.

A paralysed girl, for the last time in a man's embrace, senses a woman staring in consternation; good day, says the woman, what are you doing here, are you on a show tour? Some kind of excursion?

— I don't know anything — mumbles the soldier — I don't know anything, it had to be the square, so the square it is — his shaky legs climbing the steps, the smoked window hides the girl's blushes.

Two soldiers in battle dress furiously throw the wheelchairs onto the van; the cripples anxiously clutch the backrests of the seats; from the side street runs a soldier, out of breath; the wheelchair flies along the pavement; wait, men, please wait for us, wait; his passenger tries to cling to the speeding wheels with numb fingers, stop, wait, the engines gun, the woman turns and slowly goes away…

Czarnoleka: Black Meadow*

Shadow and silence cling to the cell; occasionally a rat prowls beneath the boards, but soon takes cover; from time to time the plumbing resounds with Eastern harmonics.

He stands with his back to the door. Before him is an iron grating; the trapped glaze of frosted air glistens between the bars; through its translucence he sees the exercise-ground, surrounded by barracks.

He stands with his back to the door; he did not go out into the yard today; he didn't have to go out into the yard today; it is one of the few things he can decide for himself, and he did not go out for exercise with the others today. The same yesterday, the same tomorrow.

The iron bars project themselves on the silhouettes of people circling the yard; each bit of grating squares its own man; he stands with his back to the door, watching.

There is a rustling sound behind the low steel door as the flap of the spy-hole is raised; but the glass has

*Czarnoleka (Black Meadow) is an illusion to Bialoleka (White Meadow), where the author and many other political detainees were held after the December 1981 declaration of martial law.

been smeared with magarine and there is no way to check what is going on inside the cell.

The key makes a hoarse, guttural sound, then the brittle voice of the bolt sounds and the door opens; the screw stands in the doorway; he had planned to do a quick search and now looks at him in halting surprise. He takes a few steps, the boards rock and sway on the rotten joists, the screw peers round the cell with his ferret's eyes.

— What's up?

— Nothing.. Just making sure the place isn't falling apart…

He walks up to the window, taps an enormous key against the windowsill, then picks up the bag abandoned on the bunk and greedily looks inside.

— What's up?

— Nothing…Just making sure the windows aren't falling apart…

He departs in a foul temper; the heavy door crashes against the frame, the steel air vibrates; he stands with his back to the door and hears the screw opening up the next cell.

He watches the prison yard through the grating; people circle round in cottonwool silence, prisoners from his cell among them. Prisoners of war.

They circle; the guards stand at the side, holding them on the leash of their eyes; their steel-grey overcoats are the colour of air and their silhouettes fade and vanish; the flat yard is intersected by crooked poles from which hangs a mesh of barbed-wire nerves and a stunted tree that will beget no leaves.

The detainees circle; criminal offenders are in the barracks opposite; packs of cigarettes fly over the net close to their windows; they hook them on pieces of board removed from the bunks — each board has a nail at the end — so the packs can be spiked and carefully hauled inside.

— When are you getting out? — they shout, and the bars do not muffle the voices. — When are you going to put an end to all this nonsense?

A guard dashes out from behind the barracks; the windows of the criminal block slam shut; the screw snatches up the cigarettes and looks scathingly at the prisoners in the yard.

— Let 'em have those fags, they're Christians too; they're better Poles and Catholics than you, they're better Poles than you, the guard stutters. A convict is pushing a wheelbarrow along the wire fence, a sweater comes flying towards him out of the window like a big shaggy bird and settles on the barbed wire; the convict delicately removes it with the haft of his spade and hides it among the concrete blocks in the barrow; he moves on, but promptly stops; the screw's clammy fingers fumble among the blocks and winkle out the garment; the prisoner stares, thinking of the punishment in store, or else with no thought at all.

He stands with his back to the door; he looks at the others dwarfed by the exercise yard and recognizes them at that distance without difficulty. He knows them.

The one who has stood still for a moment, looking towards the watchtower, is a famous old partisan; after World War Two, he specialized in breaking up Stalinist jails. He freed many people. But he will never succeed in smashing the prison where he is now ensnared. He was given seven death sentences — three were waived by amnesty. But he is still alive; he continues his walk, he is circling the yard.

That mousy one with thick specs and a hearing aid went deaf in Siberia where his mother gave birth to him. After concentration camp she was sentenced to lifelong deportation and didn't even teach her son Polish; they said he'd never have any use for it. When they came back he was several years old. In Moscow they had stood in a long gloomy line; she wanted him to have a look at that waxworks face. He returned, now he is circling the yard.

The stooping figure over there was once behind the barbed wire of a Nazi camp. He did not escape to freedom through the chimney; he returned by another route, he is circling the yard.

The man with the limp got a couple of years under Gomulka for a poem about the stupidity of Poles. At the trial they refused to believe that the poem was really by Jan Kochanowski. He served his time for Kochanowski, was freed, now he is circling the yard.

That fellow over there was in the Warsaw Uprising at the age of fourteen, and when Poland was liberated, he was promptly given several years in prison. The indictment they read out stated that he had attempted to overthrow the new system of social justice. The lad chatting with him is still a schoolboy; he held different views from his teachers. Both are circling the yard.

The fellow in the sailor's jacket is a poet, he circles the yard thrashing out the rhythm of a poem.

Those two workers are recalling a trade union that no longer exists. It was swept away by war, yet the newspapers said all workers wanted another union that would be the only genuine one and would meet their demands. The workers circle the yard.

That one is a printer who published the uncensored Milosz. For his work he received the writers' award. He could not collect it because he was in prison on a theft charge. He came out, but now he too is circling the yard.

That gesturing man refused to agree in 1968 that Mickiewicz should not be staged because he was anti-socialist. If he had disagreed with nothing else, he might have got away with a police thrashing. But he got several years. He came out. Now he is circling the yard.

He turns away from the window, slowly takes one step, two steps. Then another few steps between the tiered bunks. Four steps in one direction, two to the side, four back, two to the side.

He is a writer, now he is circling round the cell; together with the others he is circling, circling...

Freeze-frame Thirteen

…This conversation is being monitored…this conversation is being monitored…this conversation is being monitored…this conversation is being monitored…I am dreadfully tired, because I have been reading over a thousand pages of entries to a competition about the fate of couples a few years after their wedding and I feel completely shattered; there were several hundred entries mostly written by women, but it sounded as though they were written by a single woman, written by a single desperate woman, written by a single woman gone crazy from despair or a mythomaniac; unbelievable; all those marriages minted the same way, all those young people who talked themselves into the belief that they are basically entitled to be happy, and already the first few months, not even years, those wanderings through strange hovels costing a lot of money, living in the family flat with mother-in-law, who is always a plague, living apart and the meetings behind bushes, with a chance for a flat in the year two thousand, before retirement, children, who come into the world as if anybody needed them, a moment later and the husband starts to crack and is more and more often returning drunk; the warrior, who cannot win anything, apart from those few printed ration cards for offal, for which his woman will get her ribs broken in the queue for shoes, which are unobtainable, for soap, which is enough for a couple of days, a few ration cards for life, which one cannot buy, because there is only getting up at dawn, drudgery, queues and the television news and maybe also queuing in front of the shop overnight, a shop where once upon a time they were selling fridges, or washing machines, and later, inevitably the first time you feel the fist of your drunken husband in your face; those women would eat the carpet for a wee bit of love, but usually they do not know the word; this exotic word, which nobody will ever explain to them, because this word has been obliterated from our language, killed in cold blood, this word lov...this conversation is being monitored...this conversation is being monitored...this conversation is being monitored...this conversation is being monitored...

Breathless

The view from the window is moist and delicate, like an infinite distance in mist. But it is only a sheet stretched over the bars; it has to be doused with water, then it cools for a moment, only to be coated again in the mossy stifling steam that clings to the naked men sitting silent and breathless at the table.

The sun parches the barracks; every few minutes one of the men reaches for an aluminium mug, plunges it in the bucket, draws water and splashes it over his left shoulder on to the sheet with the gesture of someone breaking a spell.

He replaces the dented mug and returns to his thoughts without so much as a glance around, stretching automatically.

The mug stands on the windowsill, its pale whiteness blurred against the shroud over the grating; the mug is covered all over in designs and tattoos; it has been retrieved from numerous mouths, and the date stamp tells that it has been thirty-one years in service. The sides are lined with lettering, naked women, dates, article and paragraph numbers that have broken the successive owners; someone reaches out again, draws from the bucket, splashes; the water spills onto the windowsill with a metallic clang, and the man puts the cup of bitterness aside once more as though it were an ordinary object.

The naked bodies at the table are overcome by langour and sweat; they sit in silence and slowly, intently breathe an air so empty that it no longer soothes the lungs.

Two hours more to midday — that is the hour of releases; it is at this precise hour each day that luck could strike; steps will be heard in the corridor that may well stop outside this door; with a whine of bolts the screw will appear in the doorway and grudgingly call out a name and turn his back before adding, get packed.

The one whose name is called will feel his pulse suddenly quicken; how shall I pack, where to, he reassures himself out loud; perhaps I'm being transferred, maybe they've brought charges, fuck 'em; probably a transfer. Or to give evidence at a trial.

— Now is the time for discharges. They take the convoy at eight a.m. — someone at the side says — but remember, once they came on the dot of ten...

The one whose name is called will excuse himself in this manner, he will suddenly let loose a great flow of talk, feverishly gesturing towards some objects that have to be packed, towards people whose names were not called; they will have to help him, as his fingers are too numb to hold on to anything for long.

It is the hour for discharges, but no one discusses the matter out loud; the scorching heat leaves them no strength for words; words today would be too heavy to utter.

Specks of dust melt into their bodies like snow, and they are silent; those who sit with their backs to the door keep a sharp eye on those who have the door in view; they can hear better. The cell door suddenly opens without a sound as though the hot metal had gone soft and the key could turn voicelessly in the lock; the guard has his cap tilted over the back of his head, rivulets of sweat stream from under the visor and down his face; he impatiently diverts them with the back of his palm.

He stands in the doorway looking at the seated men, then softly utters a surname.

The one whose name has been called rises slightly, then sits down; the screw knows that it is the hour for going free, so he persists in his silence, as though he fears the words might scald his lips.

— Well? Here I am...

The screw rubs his eyelids with the tip of his finger, from which the prison key is hanging like a huge wedding ring; he presses his eyelids carefully to verify that his eyes are still there, and speaks softly into his palms.

— For cross-examination.

The one whose name has been called now takes gentle breaths, he reaches for the aluminium mug, draws from the bucket.

— I'm not going for cross-examination.

— No?

— No.

He splashes water over the back of his shoulder and quickly sets aside the mug, which the water has not had time to cool.

— Who'd beat his meat in this heat. I'm not going.

The screw stays put; he should have moved on, slamming the burning-hot door, but he stands on the threshold, and a pale man appears from behind his shoulders; his face as white as if the blood had drained out of him; won't you talk to me either? Eh? Don't you want to talk to me?

The one whose name has been called rises slowly, mechanically, without so much as a thought; he stands up, takes a few steps; but only as far as the door; he reaches for his shirt, which was wilting on the bunk, and he turns uncertainly around.

— My father — he says with an effort to the men seated at the table.

The door today is like rubber and emits no sound.

— Then I'll water the cloth. Until he returns.

— He said his father worked for the secret police. It was his first visit. They're not in contact. He didn't come on any of the visitors' days.

— So he gets a special visit. Took him unawares. That's why he went. They're not in contact. He went in a state of total confusion.

— He thought he was going to freedom. It's the time of day.

The thick felt of heat smothers their words, time ebbs and flows in all directions.

The cigarette smoke soaks up the last streams of air. The hour of freedom has not yet elapsed, and they feel its every tremor.

— Might as well tap next door. May someone's going out today.

— We'd hear if they did.

They are silent; the smouldering fag-ends corrode the metal of the tin, they sense the soft footsteps that cannot be heard from the corridor, the door moves in the salt-dry dust of the air, and the one whose name was called is standing in the doorway.

He throws his shirt back on the bunk; the sleeve slides slowly floorwards; he takes several steps; but only so far as the table; he picks up the mug, draws water from the bucket, splashes some onto the rag and drenches his hair with the rest, then seats himself on a stool.

— It was my father, he says at some speed, I told you my father works for the secret police. I have no contact at all with him. He did not come visiting because he knew I wouldn't want to speak to him. He took me unawares. That's why I went. I have no contact with him at all. I went in a state of total confusion...

— But it was a brief encounter...

The one whose name was called pulls a shrivelled cigarette from the pack and runs his tongue along the paper hull, leaving no trace of moisture. He rolls the cigarette in his finger; tobacco spills from under his nails.

— It wasn't an extra visit. It was a routine interrogation. There was another screw sitting there and they both wanted to cross-examine me.

He lights the cigarette, and its empty casing sparks with yellowish glimmers.

— My father screamed at me that I'm a fool to be inside here in this scorcher and that he can fix my release any time just so long as I sign the pledge of loyalty, and the other geezer said they need men like me to work with them, not sit in the jug.

— I said I refused to speak to them because they have blood on their hands. The other fellow blew his top and stormed out. I walked out too. My father yelled after me that I'm a fool and to stop being a fool, that he'd give me a colour TV as a peace offering. He never came visiting. He took me unawares. That's why I went. I have no contact with him at all. I went in a state of total confusion. I told them I refused to talk to them because they have blood on their hands. The other fellow blew his top and stormed out. I told you my father works for the secret police. He yelled after me that I'm a fool and to stop being a fool, that he'd give me a colour TV as a peace offering...

— Light up — one of them said and handed him a smouldering fag. — Light up. And then you can tell us everything...

— I have no contact...

— Light your fag. And douse the sheet.

The one whose name had been called reaches for the mug, but his hand is off the mark, and he has to turn round to measure his aim. Then he draws water from the bucket and splashes it over his shoulder; the piece of sheet is stiff as tin; the drops trickle down like mercury and patter against the windowsill.

The hour of discharges is coming irrevocably to a close; calm and resignation slowly spread among them, and the sensory threads that link them with the corridor begin one after the other to break.

And then the corridor suddenly returns to life; it fills with voices, bolts clap, footsteps approach.

— What's up? What's the row?

One of them stoops close to the door, avidly catches at the alarming, all but undecipherable sounds.

— Perhaps someone's being discharged? I wonder. Tap next door.

The wall gives no reply; don't rap now, someone says, the screw's in there, wait a bit.

— They seem to be coming here — says the fellow by the door and takes a step back, the metal plate quivers on the door and stills; a man stands in the metal-framed threshold, with his shoulders all but propped against the plate, for the door has slammed behind him in an instant.

He stands dead-still and distrustfully inhales the unfamiliar air; in his hands he holds a bundle wrapped in a grey blanket, on which he precariously balances an aluminium bowl containing an aluminium plate and an engraved, dented aluminium mug; the sides are lined with lettering, naked women, dates, article and paragraph numbers that have broken the successive owners — Where're you from? he asks from the doorway.

— Here and there — the men at the table reply. — How about yourself?

— I'm a lecturer. They've brought in a whole convoy of us.

— Of university types?

— No. A mixed bunch, they've just brought us, the place is chock-a-block. Have you been inside long? — he asks uncertainly.

— Pleased to meet you, prof. That bunk's free. Put your baggage down and take a peg.

— What baggage?

— That thing you're holding in your hands. Your bundle. Sit down, relax. Then you can tell us about yourself.

— Warm, isn't it? — the prof says slowly.

— Is that all you've got? Apart from state property?

— For months I'd kept a bag ready with all my stuff. Today was the first time I didn't take it with me. And they picked me up from the college. Have you been in here long?...

— Not that long, coming up to six months.

The prof sits on the bunk; the objects in the aluminium bowl rattle.

— How much longer will you be...

He rests his elbows on his knees, and his head inclines readily towards his palms.

They wait for him patiently, in silence.

— Things had got so much better of late; everything was sorting itself out, with the wife we were making a bit on the side, we were beginning to make ends meet; my wife works in the same institute where I'm a lecturer; a friend chucked it all in and started an artistic metalwork studio, he put us in the way of a tidy penny, gave us metal flowers to paint; after putting the children to bed my wife did the heads, and I added a splash of green; after a couple of nights' practice it went like a bomb, like a bomb...we began to recoup a little financially...we even started planning a holiday...I'd kept that bag ready for months...bitch of a world...

The hour of discharges is passed beyond recall; the one whose name had been called now reaches for the mug and knocks it impatiently on the bottom of the bucket.

— I'd kept that bag ready for months...it was going like a bomb...like a bomb...

Freeze-frame Fourteen

…The taxi driver passes his home; standing at the front door is his wife; he stops the cab and opens for her; the woman sits in silence; in old age you've become so boring, it makes me puke; he looks at her with vindictive satisfaction; I'll go to the hairdresser and have my hair dyed Chestnut No. 5, shouts the desperate woman, sure that she'll change her life; have your ass dyed Chestnut No. 5, he answers soothingly; you bastard, have you seen a broad with a prick; what broad, what are you talking about; if you can't see, then you'd better look at your wedding picture; she slams the door, and he pulls away; both of them will have a fine day.

Why does the old man spit in the face of the young one who jostled him?

Why does the pregnant woman, who tried to jump the queue at the butcher's to get a piece of meat, stumble out of the shop, tears rolling down on to her prominent stomach, and the words coming after her to trip her swollen legs: shouldn't have screwed around, wouldn't have a belly-full now, you…

Why does the doctor twist the old woman's arm and back while shoving her out of his office?

The hatred cultivated in the people of this country does not allow them to think; the unrelenting hunt for victims leaves no time for it, and the government really no longer needs to reform the nation…

Prison Sickness

The night's silence runs cold in the cell. Motionless shadows wilt on the walls.

The window grating is overgrown with a thick mesh that guards the inside and suppresses sounds. The loathsome Alsatian can't be heard — it thrashes about between the fence of thorn and the sky-high wall, which is daubed over with white paint to the height of a prisoner's upraised arms. The paint flakes off, baring previous layers of the Gomulka and Gierek eras; it is a young prison.

Bitter stars spilling out of the narrow tape of sky cannot squeeze through the steel mesh.

A scant rustling sound can be heard the other side of the low metal doors. The screw eavesdrops for a while, then delicately raises the tin shutter of the spyhole and peers in. There in the even darkness bunks are stacked high. The grey fold of a blanket slides to the floor. Someone's palm shows white. The warped aluminium mug absorbs the faint gleam from the other side of the window.

The luminous spot on the sheet-metal door fades out. The screw has done his duty; he won't be overlooked for promotion.

He lies motionless, supporting his head on his numbed

hand; he really should change position. Instead he moves his head only slightly, taking in the cell with his gaze; and now he sees the grating with its metal veil and the high prickly hedge beyond, the other side of which is a strip of meticulously raked desert sand and the hound and that wall, daubed over in white paint to the height of a prisoner's upraised arms. The wall is searched by a probing light; under the glare white paint flakes off without a sound...

He lies motionless. The stillness is disrupted by voices floating over from the barracks, which is invisible through the grating. They soak through the grating and reverberate from the walls, pillars and bends. The other block is at communal prayer. The prisoners open all the windows and garbled words mix confusedly in the night, amid which snatches of songs, hymns and choruses float out like bubbles and burst. Again the prisoners can't agree on a single version: Father — Lord God Thou'rt Poland — Poland's not perished yet — we'll not desert — as long as Poles — God rest their souls — the priest chased Katie — the crow won't the eagle — whence our nation came — we shall regain — dragged out by night — ...After a moment the bazaar of voices drifts away like a frigate on the wind, and now only single words flutter in the mesh; the hound slinks off with its tail tucked under.

He lies motionless. His head slides off his hand and he instantly feels sharp little needles of blood darting into his fingers, which slowly return to life. He begins to move his fingers. He moves his hand between the folds of the blanket and chances on some scraps of paper and envelopes and bookcovers. The colour that he now touches is cool and thick: the blue binding of a notebook

109

from which the inside was ripped out a few hours back during the search. The covers are now without the written pages, but some vestiges and fragments of jotted sentences and words still swirl in their midst, cling to them: two worlds — a shop trainee showers people standing in line with orangeade and hides, laughing, behind the empty shelves; no one reacts; many newspapers carry reports on the bear that has shown up in the Tatra, it is affectionately referred to as teddy, and a special correspondent reports on it for the Express; on Polish radio there's a program "Teatime round the Samovar", Polevoy, editor-in-chief of *Yunost*, is dreaming of a trip to Eastern Siberia, he tells the legend of how Siberia was created by God, who felt tired one day and tipped out a whole bagful of wealth, he also tells how the Germans wanted to blow up the monastery on Jasna Gora and put the blame on the Russians, the Russians however found out about this diabolical plan and thank God, as Polevoy puts it, saved the monastery; a man in the shop stuffed a frozen goose under his shirt, you won't squeal, he asks his neighbour in the line; mister, they must come, sure as two and two is four, they'll come for sure, ask anyone you like, they want to anyway, they fucking well do, they'll leave only stones behind, they must come in the end, those Chinks; we average women ought always to be cheerful; assent to falsehood is the root of evil in the country — from the testament of Ryszard Siwiec of Przemysl: lawyer and soldier in the Home Army, who set fire to himself in the stadium during Gomulka's speech at the harvest festival; he was protesting against the invasion of Czechoslovakia; one thousand eight hundred tons of powdered milk from West Germany forwarded to prisons and old people's homes on the contention that they contain dangerous hormones; the institute that issued the pronouncement turned out not to have the equipment for such tests; Norwid — where energy out-distances intelligence, there's a massacre every genera-tion; a criminal prisoner, a robber turned trusty, sixth year inside, says a good thing we've got martial law, there'll be some order at last, lately a fellow was afraid even to go out onto the street; Marek, already nodding off on his bunk, in a state of half-sleep, once I'm in Canada the first thing I'll do is go to a shop, you can get everything in the shops there, and I'll buy myself a kilo of communism and every evening I'll give it a fucking great battering with a hammer, till the day I die; those empty notebook covers; scraps of jotted sentences slowly fade, the covers grow cold and harden, and a vigilant plain-clothes policeman is now bent over a wad of torn-out pages.

He lies motionless, the numb hand slowly regains feel-ing, painfully, as after a bout of prison sickness, but the head does not move; half-dropped eyelids; he can just see the man behind the bars; the blind light from above the wall presses through the window and projects a shadow of the lad who climbs gingerly down from the upper bunk so as not to wake the cripple sleeping beneath; he's reached the floor now, for the bunks, arranged on rotten planks, begin to shake; he raises the lid of the bucket, draws some coffee and drinks avidly; the warm stimulant diffuses lazily through his veins; the man pauses and stands stock-still, straining his ears; out in the corridor he hears a key rattling in the lock of the grating which separates this corridor from the duty-room; the grating drops and the screw won't be

111

able to open it again until morning, as the key is taken from him for the night; he won't appear in the corridor again this shift. A stormy day ends on the consumptive rattle of iron bars; when hours ago two inmates were led out on their successive journeys into the unknown, several hundred men began to bang their aluminium dishes against the bars; that orgy of sounds, unending, in a vacuum disrupted by the prison siren wailing its alarm call; those who're in cells at the wall end and don't know what's going on in the yard, listen greedily; the din of vibrating dishes dies violently down, the cell door opens suddenly and a gang of police crashes in; their helmeted heads make them look like motorcyclists on their way to a country ball; the short-legged captain punctuates his words with his white baton; we've put up with so much so long, it's all up now, we'll give you a fucking what for, see, a right fucking what for, see, all out now, hurry; greedy hands in the corridor fumble bodies and tear at clothes, a hob-nailed foot is raised as if to give a kick in the belly, but the energetic boot merely strips the trousers off instead; the man now stands naked; a camera is heard to hiccough; one of the motorcyclists has put his baton aside and takes photos, others charge into the cell and hide behind the doors.

Afterwards the cell is alien and inaccessible. They slowly enter, pause; blankets, clothes, papers and books are stacked on the bunks, the scrap of cable and two razor blades that could be connected to the light flex for boiling water have vanished; the cupboard has spilled out its guts and helplessly spreads its wings, an onion rolls about on the floor. The place now seems strange, one must first re-acclimatize before one can restore remembered shapes, as after a forced move.

He had then sat on the bunk, leaned his head on his hand, and when night came, no one in the cell let him know.

The other man burrows into his bunk and falls silent; a transparent vein of light collects flickering beads of dust; his hand, now restored, wanders through the dunes of the blanket; his fingers encounter rustling pages, stray among words so familiar that they can be read from the relief of the letters; what can I write you, how can I write you, I'm seldom in Warsaw, this town is hell; so are others, only different; I feel that without our meetings in Przechodnia Street an important point has ceased to exist in my mental geography; would you like any books, how about some English ones; learn a language, because otherwise you'll go mad; well then, Lopucha has sat down to write you a letter twice already, she sat down, gripped her pen, the paper's on the table, and then what, nothing came of it; wondering what could, what would, and nothing comes into her head; and now I drink to your health, your good spirits and Wyspianski's "Liberation"; it's so difficult to write to you, because I don't know how one writes to people who've come a cropper, who can't break loose from their own thoughts; then there's always the question whether what we are doing has any sense; by the way, I should mention that the Metropolitan Commander of the Citizens' Militia has no influence on the function- ing of the postal services, nor therefore on the times at which mail is delivered; he sits up on the bunk for the first time in hours; first sweeps up everything around him, then fishes out from the pile books, shirts, letters, socks, a matchbox, photographs, bird feathers, a sweater; with precise movements he sets all his belongings in the old places he had so far been unable to retrieve in his memory. Then he smoothes out the blanket, chances on a cigarette in its folds, lights it, quietly descends from the bunk and calmly pees into the bucket.

He sits down by the table to smoke and shakes the ash over his left shoulder outside the bars.

He is smoking, then reaches to where the empty tin always used to stand and where the lump of margarine always lay; he fills the tin with margarine, reaches round his neck and rips the strap off his prison shirt, pushes it into the margarine; a match flickers. The tin comes suddenly to life, as though a swarm of luminous white ants had come seething out of it; he reaches under the bunk to the place where the cardboard box always used to be and screens the pulsing source of life from those who are sleeping.

He sits at the table; on the box is an exotic label: the name of some Paris factory, shop or institution with the address and telephone number. Avenue Franco-Russe — he recalls that street from a previous life; the Franco-Russian street, it intersects avenue Rapp; that is where the gasline is supposed to end; one day the red Siberian gas will gush out and suffocate all the pathetic fools who have done nothing to deserve their city.

He reaches for the binding where the notebook always used to be; he opens it, silently. Those scraps of sentences and words, now irretrievably locked within his card-index, appear and return, jostling their way back, they're there.

Just another stretch of the arm to where the piece of paper always lay and where it lies again; it's covered on one side in print — a list of things from the Austrian parcels that were distributed here by the Polish Red Cross; the Austrian National Committee for Aid to Polish Detainees, gifts of the Austrian Red Cross. A sanitary package for women. One soap, 1 toothpaste, 1 washing powder, 1 shampoo, 1 package for female hygiene, 250 grams of cottonwool.

He turns the sheet over, it glints with dazzling whiteness; then he takes a ballpoint from his pocket and stoops over the wick to prevent the glow shimmering on the pane and arousing the guard who watches behind his back in the high tower above the wall.

He leans forward.

The night's silence runs cold in the cell. Motionless shadows wilt on the walls.

The window grating is overgrown with a thick mesh that guards the inside and suppresses sounds. The loathsome Alsatian can't be heard — it thrashes about between the fence of thorn and the sky-high wall, which is daubed over with white paint to the height of a prisoner's upraised arms. The paint flakes off, baring previous layers of the Gomulka and Gierek eras; it is a young prison.

Bitter stars...

Freeze-frame Fifteen

…The alien railway station, ceiling vanishing somewhere into the heights, feet cold on the stone floor; no hopeful goodbyes or greetings bring relief.

Sly cameras shamelessly stare into faces, deaf tunnels greedily swallow people up, the air has a regular beat.

The jealous information windows are mum; an unobtrusive queue hugs the wall by the newspaper stand with its loud titles: *Merry-Go-Round, Land of Soviets, My Home, World of the Deaf, Poland, Party Life, Nutrition, Let's Live Longer, Soviet Woman, Poland with Wings, Livestock Breeding, From the Battle Front, Literaturnaya Gazyeta, For and Against, Poland in Russian, Here and Now, Problems of Peace and Socialism* (Russian edition), *The Woodland Voice, Do-It-Yourself, Soviet Lights, Mental Health, Public Health, Generation, Pig Breeding, Together, At Friends, Defence Knowledge, Izvestia, Discover the World, For Freedom and People, Intensive Therapy, Young Communist Pravda*. The soldiers' weapons shine, and their hob-nailed boots echo.

A roar rises to fill the ceiling; carriages spill out gangs of reservists with eyes white from vodka; they throng the platforms, clinging to each other, stunned by the illusion of freedom, bloodied in numerous skirmishes; gaudy banners whisk about, giving dates, platoon numbers and localities; a nervous patrol, which stretches an invisible string along the platforms, turns a blind eye. Yells of demobbed at last, more than one cunt shed a tear, the howls echo; the reservists, who have already fulfilled their commendable December duties, mix with

116

the conscripts, stupified by drink; their vacant eyes search for the right trains, which will take them towards their new functions and duties. *Mama, come to my induction,/Sergeant-Major sends his card;/Bum grenade blew my hand off,/Come and see, this is your blood.* Bellowing of drunken throats; a train draws out, a conscript hanging out of a window, and the vomit streams along the car like an azure veil; a drunken girl flings herself after the carriage, whimpering. She runs, her bluish calves flicker; crashing into a pylon, she slides down, leaving on the concrete a trail of blood, phlegm and tears...

Postscript — 1985

Empty...Sort of

The taxi driver went up to the duty-room on cottonwool legs and stood quietly before the blurred pane with the round aperture. He twirled his cap in his hands and looked coaxingly at the duty-officer, who sat with his head collapsed on his chest. He looked like a man overcome by insurmountable drowsiness. But he was simply stooped over a small mirror set on his knee. A scrap of newspaper with a rosette of coagulated blood stuck to his upper lip; he was delicately trying to prize it away with the nail of his little finger.

— Excuse me, Sir, if you please.. — said the taxi driver, as he bowed low and froze in timeless obeisance.

The duty-officer shuddered and violently raised his head. The congealed drop of blood remained on his nail, a soft clank resounded under the table, and simultaneously atoms of light flashed in the semi-darkness.

— Seven years' bad luck — the taxi driver sheepishly volunteered, but was instantly scared by his own voice. The duty-officer looked at him, but manifested no irritation, as the scarlet streak that now joined the gash to the corner of his mouth caused him to smile rapaciously with half of his face.

— Well? — the duty-officer spoke. — Wha'?

— How to.. — the taxi driver at one jerk whipped off his cap — How to...I mean...is there any other exit?

— Wha'?

— I've got a passenger here, tall, cap, overcoat, I mean...said he'd be gone two minutes, but my meter's already clocked up a thousand seven hundred...and it's chilly...so maybe there's another exit here, or how...

— No one of that description came in 'ere today — the duty-officer said, grinding the glass with his boot.

— What d'ya mean no one of that description, when I saw him go in with my own eyes — for a moment the taxi driver lost his head, then instantly simmered down — I saw him go in. Cap and overcoat. Eight a.m. What time's it now? A thousand seven hundred on the meter. Chilly...isn't there another exit here, or...

— No one of that description came in 'ere today. Wait 'ere quietly or else go home. What I says I says. Yes or no. Got it?

The bewildered taxi driver reeled towards the door; what d'ya mean, no one came in when I saw him go in, had an overcoat, said stay put and wait, what d'ya mean when I tell you I saw him go in...it's like a movie, dammit, like a movie...a cap...

Two people passed him who without looking round proceeded along the familiar route to the blurred pane with the aperture. The taxi driver eyed them suspiciously and retreated to the door; it'll soon make a thousand seven hundred and forty — seven hundred and forty. Cold, eh?

The two men then tackled the stairs, the repellent metal netting climbed upwards above the banisters. The duty-officer sat behind the glass, staring down at the floor, at the carmine mouth of the actress whose photo had come unstuck from the broken mirror. One might have thought he was blowing on his cold fingers. But he was only holding the receiver in his huge palm and reporting in dulcet tones — It's the, it's them two literary blokes summoned for...

And now they were instinctively but unnecessarily raising their heads to read the nameplates fastened above the doors, as they made their unerring way to the correct one.

They stopped outside, and when one of them raised his hand to knock, the door slid away from his fingers. For a moment they stood eye to eye, saying nothing, then they heard the instruction: I'm too busy right now, kindly wait on that bench for a while, we can have a chat later; they turned away towards the bench, retreating under an escort of eyes. Then they sat down and simultaneously leaned back on the bench as though a gust of wind from the closed doors had pushed them there.

They were silent, and the hard keyboard of the typewriter could be heard rattling away from the other side of the door.

Then for a long time the glow-lamp hissed beneath the ceiling, regularly died down, then returned after a moment. One of them took a newspaper from his pocket and glanced at the door, the other twirled a cigarette in his fingers spilling bits of tobacco, then placed it in his mouth without lighting up. They sat in silence, hemmed in by words that had already erupted earlier that day, on their way to this place.

They had been standing in a tramcar that dragged itself across the bridge so slowly the water beneath did not stir; it was in the paper, one of them said, about reducing the speed limit, people are inconvenienced by the noise, which in our language means the bridge is in danger of collapse; then the tram stopped and the door-wings flapped; smoke was belching from under the first wagon and when they go out, they saw a little woman in a tram conductor's cap rampaging down the car and yelling to the passengers, run for your lives, it'll be a right balls-up un' I don't know who's gunna pay, and as though to emphasize her words she banged the fire extinguisher on the asphalt; the extinguisher emitted a prolonged whistle, then after the last thump the bottom fell out, spilling a handful of rust from inside; people peered curiously under the car and for the first time that day their faces were creased with laughter; it's a sight for sore eyes, they whispered among themselves, smoking like the devil. They made for the river bank walking slowly, watching the exuberant water below; they passed the bays and the bridge ebbed away — I've never been so hamstrung by censorship as now, never; for the last couple of years it's been different, especially now; the old censor could be fooled in thousands of ways; the game could be fun, could be humiliating, but I don't know how to tackle this one; he's inside me, and he keeps getting stronger; he was pretty strong way back in '80 and '81, but in those days you simply waited, you could still suppress all your inner doubts; my censor made himself known in earnest when I was in jail; all those previously diffuse and elusive elements were concentrated in one place, several hundred people; it was a colony of apes; at first I resisted that image and rejected my own evaluation, but then the image took hold; besides, I wasn't alone. They hauled in a sober-minded bloke from the Poly and after a couple of days, he realized how nauseated I was by all that jingoism, all that ritual and religious singing every day through the bars, stirring up the entire prison to a hunger strike every other minute on the least pretext, and I saw great tub-thumpers who noshed at night on the quiet and broke those fasts of theirs after two days; that ranting on for months on end about high-level politics, and "the spring will be ours" even though the spring went on relentlessly; the division between those who held that the greatest service to the country was to take the mickey out of the screw and those who went to give the screws the season's greetings: that'll give 'em something to think about, they'd say, and so another month was twaddled away; plus those symbols, symbols of something that no longer existed, because people didn't have it inside them in the first place; so that sober bloke from the Poly started telling how a legend was growing up about our prison in the outside world, people were saying that the extreme of the extreme had been rounded up here; as a rank-and-file activist he was glad they'd taken him, he stood to learn a lot here in this academy of the opposition; that's what he called it, now he's just wondering how the whole business could ever have lasted sixteen months; he couldn't get over his amazement as he looked on and observed how a respectable union activist was happy if he caught sight of a secret policeman in the yard, because he could shout at him from a safe distance, you bastard, you broken prick on duck's legs; he watched and was amazed and wondered what could be gained by all that; he looked at those people who gobbled the chocolate from foreign parcels and then listened to children's stories about ration cards for two hundred grams of lemon drops, and that was an excuse for preaching about the ruthlessness of the authorities; he beheld a once-important guru whose mental laziness prevented his reassessing his view of his own importance; once he had conducted discussions about how the system encourages and fosters alcoholism, how the system depends on it, and here he had now discovered a way of distilling moonshine, and distilled it on the sly; he saw those who'd wanted to hang grafters now giving bribes to the man in charge of the baths who was serving a sentence for corruption, and for a douceur you can whistle a shirt with the prison stamp; it can be smuggled through at visiting hours; the women outside like to sport a grey shirt with the prison sign as a gesture of mourning; he saw them grumbling to the Swiss doctors from the Red Cross who've already seen a prison or two in Asia and South America; he heard them complaining that the water in the baths was too hot or too cold, he saw men who only recently had ordered others to paint graffiti about television lies, now sucking up to the screw so he'd let them watch the news out of turn; he saw politicals who treated the convicts with contempt; there were a couple of professional crooks in prison with us who went on hunger strike in sympathy, and it was entered in their personal files which would follow them through all the prisons of the land all their lives long, he saw people who were happy to be in prison and did not notice their halo was of scurf; so that sober-minded fellow told me that, though he considers himself to be a cultured type, he would formulate his view as follows — namely, he wouldn't give a shit for such an academy of opposition. Obviously not everything there was so bad, there were lots of different people, but somehow it all got blurred and that ghastly image prevailed; I ended up not writing a single word about those days, because either my censor would have made a liar of me unto death, since you simply couldn't write about such things; the idea was to build morale and boost myths regardless, and for a book like that — had I ever got round to writing — I'd have received the Ministry of Culture prize at least, or worse. Besides, what publisher would have printed it? I'd have been treated like a provocateur or police spy...

They paced their walk slowly from bay to bay, as the bridge receded, and they were soon to stand on firm, hard ground. — I find reading difficult, I pick up a book with a sense of nausea; it looks as though the garbage dump will become literature, and nothing else will remain, all those hundreds of pages, thousands of poems, memoirs, diaries, impressions, notes, all very soulful and high-minded, those sufferings endured with slimy satisfaction; how many more years is this to be our nourishment? Those December nights, wars declared on the entire nation, nothing less would do, tanks, handcuffs, armoured cars, troops going out on the street, all those stage props, even private dreams under martial law, and children's thoughts for posterity; that specific language one is duty-bound to use if one wants to belong; it's our own newspeak; those internment camps, reds, bolshies, underground broadsheets, police ambushes, raids; even those held in unbarred rooms in vacation centres refer to them as cells and camps; loss of freedom is not enough, what matters is the rig-out; when I read all that stuff I feel like puking, there's not so much as a thought on the horizon; like throwing petrol bombs at water-cannons, and there's no breaking free, for there's no tolerance here; pathos excludes tolerance and we're getting close to using hopeless propaganda, just one step from the method and gimmicks of the other side, just one step from their mentality and stereotypes, their stultification and absolutism; one mag had the guts to discuss these problems; people started shouting that it was a secret police job and I don't know if the publication's still coming out; it all makes me puke, I've had my own small part in it, but I'll probably pack it, though it's difficult to go it alone, to hell with all this foam-beating; up-fingers is the only universally adopted program to be invariably shown — that's our form of salute...

They stopped for a moment and rested against the rail; I'd gladly toss a coin into the water, one of them said, it might help me reassess a couple of problems, for either I calmly go on considering myself the aristocrat of literature or else I finally admit that the literary backwater, that provincial homespun stuff, is me; that's really what our literature is; our whingeing behind prison bars and our obtusely menacing squeaks about the spring being ours sound like poetry to us; we have nurtured censors within us who have outstripped us and our thoughts and write on our behalf about this country; we're happy from time to time to get a parcel from abroad with a kilo of sugar, a kilo of flour and some toothpaste; we'd gladly frame the parcel as documentary proof that Europe remembers and admires Polish literature; admirable people, noble nation gone to the dogs, we describe it in our own blood, but we write on blank cards dealt out by our censor; it was this censor who prevented my writing that I didn't want any hero's testimony; everyone in my prison was handed a testimony; a souvenir for life, they said with emotion, a pass to history, they said hysterically, good typographic design and half-bound what's more...

They reached the tramstop on the bridge that joined the two banks and suddenly stopped talking, as though they felt hard ground underfoot. One of them pointed at the colossal building and the huge red flag full-sail above it, and white-capped young men milling all around. And we'll carry on about how they sit there plotting which scenario to apply, but in the event we shall die standing, not on our knees. The wheels screeched. Their tram rolled up to the stop in a veil of smoke. Clearly the woman with the conductor's cap falling over her eyes had lost heart and was now staring indifferently ahead with blank expression. They boarded and the tramcar immediately dissolved in a black fog.

Afterwards they sat in silence. One of them put his newspaper away, and the other drew out his next cigarette and crushed it between his fingers. It was the twentieth cigarette he had not lit during the long hours waiting on the bench that day.

The glow-lamp hissed beneath the ceiling, the light flared, then expired. A man in overalls appeared in the aisle. He walked swiftly towards them, and drew up suddenly in passing.

— Just a moment — he said without giving them a look.

They sprang up in surprise; two more steps, two more steps, one more, said the man, and when they had moved a little to the side he pushed the bench away. Behind it there was a small metal door in the wall, which he opened. He took a screw driver from his pocket and started fiddling among the cables, tapping the microphone head. Then he glanced at them and at the cables again and shrugged his shoulders; what the fuck do they want, he muttered, everything's OK. He slammed the metal door, pushed the bench back in place and made off. He turned round for one moment longer and flung over his shoulder, Quiet, aren't we?

Then the door opened and there stood the man who'd ordered them to wait. As it happens, he said I'm quite snowed under, so we might as well call it a day. Should the occasion arise, then of course…He tapped his finger against the door-frame and closed the door behind him.

Exhausted and relieved, they went downstairs slowly; I began to feel the urge, one of them said, it's a neat situation to describe, but I thought you might want to. They descended to the landing and turned into the broad staircase; I did have the urge, only I thought less in terms of situation than of storyline, besides I thought I'd let you have it as you might feel inclined, the second one said, and that we'd sort it out between us when we left…

And they both started laughing and laughing, and they came to the room where the duty-officer sat behind the blurred aperture, and still they were laughing; the pale taxi driver stood muttering to himself by the wall; he must have come in, I saw him with my own eyes, I've clocked up four thousand two hundred, four and two hundred; you definitely didn't see him, he shouted to the duty-officer in despair. But the latter looked at the men laughing, pulled the visor over his eyes and lifted his head, because he could now see them only knee-high.

— What're ya laughin' at, huh? Who 're ya laughin' at?

— Ourselves — one of them replied.

Quietly they closed the heavy door behind them.

— Well — the duty-officer shook his fist after

them. — Well. Loonies, eh? — he turned to the taxi driver.

— No, no, it's from Gogol — the taxi driver instinctively mumbled.

About the translators: NINA TAYLOR is an Oxford trained expert in Slavic languages, now based in London. She writes and lectures on Polish literature. ANDREW SHORT is the pseudonym of a London-based specialist in Polish affairs.

STANISLAW BARANCZAK is a Polish poet and writer who was the co-founder of KOR (the Committee for the Defense of Workers) in 1976 and was an editor of the Polish underground literary quarterly *Zapis*. Since 1981 he has been teaching at Harvard University in the United States, where he is now the Alfred Jurzykowski Professor of Polish Language and Literature.

Books from
Readers International

Sipho Sepamla, *A Ride on the Whirlwind*. This novel by one of South Africa's foremost black poets is set in the 1976 Soweto uprisings. "Not simply a tale of police versus rebels," said *World Literature Today*, "but a bold, sincere portrayal of the human predicament with which South Africa is faced." Hardback only, 244 pages. Retail price, US$12.50/£7.95 U.K.

Yang Jiang, *A Cadre School Life: Six Chapters*. Translated from the Chinese by Geremie Barmé and Bennett Lee. A lucid, personal meditation on the Cultural Revolution, the ordeal inflicted on 20 million Chinese, among them virtually all of the country's intellectuals. "Yang Jiang is a very distinguished old lady; she is a playwright; she translated Cervantes into Chinese...She lived through a disaster whose magnitude paralyzes the imagination...She is a subtle artist who knows how to say less to express more. Her *Six Chapters* are written with elegant simplicity." (Simon Leys, *The New Republic*) "An outstanding book, quite unlike anything else from 20th-century China...superbly translated." (*The Times Literary Supplement*). Hardback only, 91 pages. Retail price, $9.95/£6.50.

Sergio Ramírez, *To Bury Our Fathers*. Translated from Spanish by Nick Caistor. A panoramic novel of Nicaragua in the Somoza era, dramatically recreated by the country's leading prose artist. Cabaret singers, exiles, National Guardsmen, guerillas, itinerant traders, beauty queens, prostitutes and would-be presidents are the characters who people this sophisticated, lyrical and timeless epic of resistance and retribution. Paperback only, 253 pages. Retail price $8.95/£5.95.

Antonio Skármeta, *I Dreamt the Snow Was Burning*. Translated from Spanish by Malcolm Coad. A cynical country boy comes to Santiago to win at football and lose his virginity. The last days before the 1973 Chilean coup turn his world upside down. "With its vigour and fantasy, undoubtedly one of the best pieces of committed literature to emerge from Latin America," said *Le Monde*. 220 pages. Retail price, $14.95/£8.95 (hardback) $7.95/£4.95 (paperback).

Emile Habiby, *The Secret Life of Saeed, the Ill-Fated Pessoptimist*. Translated from the Arabic by Salma Khadra Jayyusi and Trevor Le Gassick. A comic epic of the Palestinian experience, the masterwork of a leading Palestinian journalist living in Israel. "...landed like a meteor in the midst of Arabic literature..." says Roger Hardy of *Middle East* magazine. Hardback only, 169 pages. Retail price, $14.95/£8.95.

Ivan Klíma, *My Merry Mornings*. Translated from Czech by George Theiner. Witty stories of the quiet corruption of Prague today. "Irrepressibly cheerful and successfully written" says the London *Financial Times*. Original illustrations for this edition by Czech artist Jan Brychta. Hardback, 154 pages. Retail price $14.95/£8.95.

Fire From the Ashes: Japanese stories on Hiroshima and Nagasaki, edited by Kenzaburo Oe. The first-ever collection in English of Stories by Japanese writers showing the deep effects of the A-bomb on their society over forty years. Hardback, 204 pages. Retail price $14.95/£8.95.

Linda Ty-Casper, *Awaiting Trespass: a Pasión*. Accomplished novel of Philippine society today. During a Passion Week full of risks and pilgrimages, the Gil family lives out the painful search of a nation for reason and nobility in irrational and ignoble times. 180 pages. Retail price $14.95/£8.95 (hardback), $7.95/£3.95 (paperback).

Janusz Anderman, *Poland Under Black Light*. Translated from Polish by Nina Taylor and Andrew Short. A talented young Polish writer, censored at home and coming into English for the first time, compels us into the eerie, Dickensian world of Warsaw under martial law. 150 pages. Retail price $12.50/£7.95 (hardback), $6.95/£3.95 (paperback).

Marta Traba, *Mothers and Shadows*. Translated from Spanish by Jo Labanyi. Out of the decade just past of dictatorship, torture and disappearances in the Southern Cone of Latin America comes this fascinating encounter between women of two different generations which evokes the tragedy and drama of Argentina, Uruguay and Chile. "Fierce, intelligent, moving" says *El Tiempo* of Bogotá. 200 pages. Retail price $14.95/£8.95 (hardback), $7.95/£3.95 (paperback).

Osvaldo Soriano, *A Funny, Dirty Little War*. Translated from Spanish by Nick Caistor. An important novel that could only be published in Argentina after the end of military rule, but which has now received both popular and critical acclaim — this black farce relives the beginnings of the Peronist "war against terrorism" as a bizarre and bloody comic romp. 150 pages. Retail price $12.50/£7.95 (hardback), $6.95/£3.95 (paperback).

READERS INTERNATIONAL publishes contemporary literature of quality from Latin America and the Caribbean, the Middle East, Asia, Africa and Eastern Europe. Many of these books were initially banned at home: READERS INTERNATIONAL is particularly committed to conserving literature in danger. Each book is current — from the past 10 years. And each is new to readers here. READERS INTERNATIONAL is registered as a not-for-profit, tax-exempt organisation in the United States of America.

If you wish to know more about Readers International's series of contemporary world literature, please write to 503 Broadway, 5th Floor, New York, NY 10012, USA; or to the Editorial Branch, 8 Strathray Gardens, London NW3 4NY, England. Orders in North America can be placed directly with Readers International, Subscription/Order Department P.O. Box 959, Columbia, Louisiana 71418, USA.

158 TX2-FM 6046
LLK 39001-67   EE: